England's Gardens
A Modern History

England's Gardens
A Modern History

Stephen Parker

previous page *Perennial borders at St Giles House, Dorset, designed by Jane Hurst*

above *Tom Stuart-Smith's Middle Terrace at Broughton Grange, Oxfordshire*

A nation of gardeners

For centuries, the role of the garden has been intertwined with English identity. More than "a nation of shopkeepers", England is a nation of gardeners, who have long used horticulture to express who they are. Why then, in so many garden histories, is the role of society and culture overlooked? No garden is created in isolation, so this book is an attempt to position English gardens within this wider context, in order to understand who made them, and why.

On becoming a garden historian, I became fascinated by this bigger picture. All great gardens have individuality – a personality, if you like. So I wanted to learn more not only about the style and significance of each garden, but about its creators: what motivated, inspired, or influenced them? What was their story? It is these people that bring colour and substance to garden history. I remember my first visit to the magnificent Sissinghurst in Kent (see p.118), one of the most famous gardens in England. I loved it, but I wanted to know more about its makers; I could not see any divide between the creators, Vita Sackville-West and her husband Harold Nicolson, and the garden they created. Harold: master of structure and formality, creating the "bones" of Sissinghurst. Vita: the genius plantswoman, filling it with schemes that are by turns romantic and restrained. His sense of dignity – born of his military background and his discretion in his affairs with men – pervades the garden's design, while her outrageous personal life – which included very public affairs with the writers Virginia Woolf and Violet Trefusis – is reflected in the garden's vibrant hues and thrilling abundance.

Sissinghurst is just one example of how a garden is rarely its creator's sole passion. Throughout history, gardens have been marked by the concerns of their makers, be these political, cultural, social, artistic, or gender-related. The formal gardens of the 17th century were heavily influenced by spectacular French and Italian styles (see p.32) and the need for men to wield power over nature (see p.14). These were succeeded by the English landscape gardens (see p.40), in which formality was swept away in a bid to create an Arcadian dream inspired by the

A statue of Dionysus stands in the Nuttery at Sissinghurst in Kent, where gorgeous woodland planting emerges in spring

Grand Tour (see p.48) and Italian landscape paintings. These 18th-century gardens were status symbols, intended to underline their owners' cultural sensitivity. But what is rarely, if ever, discussed is that many new houses and gardens constructed during this period were funded by colonial expansion – money made from cotton, sugar, or tobacco produced by slavery, or from the trade in the enslaved people themselves. The experiences of these people were a far cry from the bucolic delights demanded by their enslavers.

Women, too, are largely ignored in garden history. It was not until the 20th century that women were recognized as serious garden makers, with the likes of Gertrude Jekyll (see p.106), Beatrix Havergal (see p.127), and Vita Sackville-West (see p.119) leading the charge. The modern era also saw new ways of living come to the fore. As the country became more industrialized, the need for green spaces in urban areas became urgent, pioneered in the public parks of the 19th century by designers such as John Claudius Loudon (see p.84). The 20th century saw the democratization of gardens, with council houses and Garden Cities offering everyday folk their own patch of land (see p.134), while the new media of radio and television explained what to do with them (see p.139).

Today, garden design has never looked healthier, with fresh-faced stars, innovative ideas, and new – and old – influences all in the mix, but it must also reckon with the unprecedented challenges posed by climate change. This is inspiring some truly exciting solutions, from the vertical gardens of London's Mayfair (see p.205) to the sustainable Cambridge Central Mosque (see p.203) and the urban regreening projects of Sheffield (see p.202).

Gardens are fascinating and wonderful however you choose to engage with them. They can simply be beautiful, but they can also tell us so much about the world we live in and the history of our culture. We are always being told that this garden is genius, or that one is insignificant, but I have always believed there is only one interpretation that matters, and that is your own.

I believe, too, that garden history should be accessible. So please use this book as you wish: as a buffet of information, as inspiration, or as a guide to enjoying a garden experience for yourself. Above all, it seeks to entice others onto the garden-history journey. I hope it sparks many further adventures for you.

top left *Beatrix Havergal with her students at the Chelsea Flower Show, 1950;* **top right** *The famous herbaceous border at Havergal's gardening college, Waterperry;* **bottom right** *Portrait of Gertrude Jekyll, 1912;* **bottom left** *Jekyll's fabulous South Border at Munstead Wood, Surrey*

the making

of the

english

"What skill and care is requyred in the sowing
and workmanly ordring..."

Thomas Hill, The Gardener's Labyrinth, *1577*

garden

Early publishing

"The garden is a ground plot for the mind,
as for pleasure and delight..."

Thomas Hill, The Gardener's Labyrinth, *1577*

England is often referred to as a "nation of gardeners", with its fine gardens, great designers, and history of influential theorists and critics. But when did this love affair begin? And where did the early garden makers find inspiration and guidance?

The first English books on gardening date from the 16th century and were largely geared towards practical information as well as some design tips. These works were revolutionary: they were among the first to be published in the English language rather than in Latin or Greek, bringing knowledge and skills that were formerly the preserve of botanists and apothecaries to a much wider audience (though still, of course, only the wealthy, literate minority).

The first garden books

William Turner, a physician as well as "the father of English botany", was very aware of the need to open up these specialist practices, and to share the medicinal properties and practical uses of plants to a readership that was not classically educated. Published in 1551, Turner's *A New Herball* was hailed as the first such treatise written in English. Despite its noble aim, the book received much criticism, as the learned elite panicked that removing barriers to knowledge would lead to its abuse by amateurs, and the diminishment of their own status as experts.

A few years later, *c.*1558, Thomas Hill would write the first book in English specifically aimed at the art of gardening. *A most briefe and pleasaunte treatise teachyng how to dresse, sowe and set a garden* offers a wealth of gardening advice, largely taken from classical writers but which Hill had kindly "englished"! In another revolutionary move, both practical and ornamental elements were discussed, creating the notion that gardens could be not only for practical use, but also for pleasure, enjoyed for their colour and scent. Though it was hardly a page-turner, the book was clearly a great success; it would be reprinted and enlarged in 1563 and again in 1568.

Hill's masterpiece, *The Gardener's Labyrinth*, would be published in 1577, under the pseudonym Didymus Mountain. It is a beautifully illustrated book that discusses a diverse range of gardening know-how, including watering, sowing, and the laying-out of those essential garden elements of the time, such as the parterre (flowerbeds arranged to form a pattern), the labyrinth, the knot garden, the wilderness, and the essential productive garden. Hill also added recipes and medicinal usage for vegetables and fruit. Such information is still pertinent today, so much so that Hill's text reads as surprisingly modern.

Eve's expulsion

In one important sense, however, these early texts were not modern at all. Turner and Hill both promulgate in their books the bizarre ancient superstition that women posed a risk to a successful garden; Hill was particularly concerned about the effect a menstruating woman might have on cucumbers, claiming that the fruits would "feeble and wyther" if she approached or handled them. Such beliefs dated back to Roman writing and had certainly been voiced by the likes of Pliny, but their origins could be traced even further back, to the very first garden, in the Bible. Just as Eve was expelled from the Garden of Eden, so the precedent was set for women to be excluded from the burgeoning business of horticulture, and it would last for centuries.

below left Botanical drawing from William Turner's A New Herball; *below right Frontispiece of Thomas Hill's* The Gardener's Labyrinth

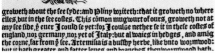

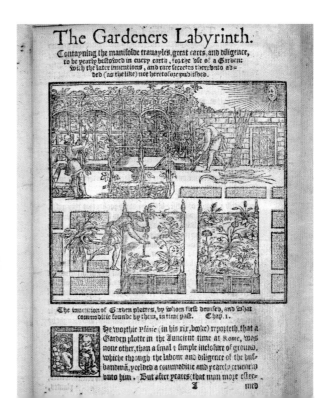

Power and nature

"It's not a palace, it's an entire city. Superb in its size, superb in its matter."

Charles Perrault, on Versailles in Le siècle de Louis le Grand, *1687*

The early English gardens were largely interpretations of the *hortus conclusus,* meaning "enclosed garden"; this was fundamentally a square or rectangular walled space in which herbs and plants could be grown both for ornamentation and medicinal purposes. Variations of this concept would evolve over the centuries, but from the accession of King Henry VIII in 1509 gardens would become a status symbol among the wealthy, with influences filtering in from across Europe to develop a much grander, more majestic version of the formal garden, with power, order, and elegance at its heart.

Status symbols

Gardens became a symbol of wealth and status for the landed elite because they were the ultimate expression of man's domination and power over nature. In garden history, this is most clearly illustrated by the garden at the 17th-century royal palace of Versailles, just west of Paris.

At first, King Louis XIV did not show much interest in Versailles, which when he came to the French throne was a small chateau that had originally been built in 1623 as a hunting lodge. However, after attending a festival thrown in his honour by the politician Nicolas Fouquet at the Château de Vaux-le-Vicomte in 1661, the king was so envious of, and threatened by, the sheer scale and opulence of Vaux that he was inspired to create a similar spectacle at Versailles – and to have Fouquet imprisoned. Already suspicious of Fouquet's obvious ambition and powerful supporters, the king was clearly threatened by this ostentatious display and

LA MAISON DE VAUX LE VICOMTE, *appartenait à Monsieur Fouquet du temps de sa surintendance, le sieur le Vveau en fut l'Architecte, elle fut commencée en 1653 et a esté mise dans sa perfection ou elle est avec une promptitude et une despence extraordinaires. Elle appartient presentement à Madame Fouquet.* A PARIS Chez N. Langlois rue à Iacque à la Victoire. Avec Privilège du Roy.
Fait par Perelle.

feared rebellion. A political power game was being playing out through parterres and planting.

The resulting gardens at Versailles, designed by the very same man who had created those at Vaux – landscape architect André Le Nôtre – were the ultimate statement of power and amazed all who were invited to visit. In a feat of pure egotism, they signified the divine rule of the Sun King and his domination over everything, including the natural world, and formality and grandeur were the perfect tools for communicating his message.

Wild abundance and natural forms were eschewed in favour of artificial shaping, man-made architectural features, and intricate patterns. Every element was massive and strictly ordered, with avenues that disappeared into the horizon, the most magnificent fountains ever seen,

the most extensive collection of sculpture anywhere, and – in a display of conspicuous religious symbolism – an almost 2.5-km (1.5-mile) cruciform canal. Like the nearby royal residence Château de Marly (now lost) and Vaux-le-Vicomte, Versailles was a supreme example of man's arrogance that he could impose total control over nature – an argument, indeed, that could be applied to gardening at all levels.

Such was the reaction to the newly aggrandized Versailles that every royal family throughout Europe sought to emulate it. The gardens were much copied, if not in scale then certainly in style, with quick-to-copy examples including the palaces of Het Loo in the Netherlands, Herrenhausen in Germany, and Peterhof in Russia, where, as at Versailles, monarchs visually asserted their status and dominion over the land – and its people. And England was no exception.

The Baroque Château de Vaux-le-Vicomte with its spectacular parterre gardens designed by André Le Nôtre

The formal Privy Gardens at Hampton Court Palace, restored in 1995 to their original 1702 plans by William III

In the decades after the Restoration of 1660, England was ruled by monarchs with French or Dutch links, and this European influence was particularly evident in the creation of their royal gardens.

A new Versailles

Following the English Civil War and Interregnum, Charles II returned from exile, where in France he had admired the magnificent gardens created by André Le Notre at Vaux-le-Vicomte and Versailles. Newly restored to the throne and with much to prove, Charles was desperate to create his own Versailles and so carried out extensive work at Hampton Court. With a smaller budget but still prioritizing size, grandeur, and ornamentation, he created 60 acres of formal pleasure gardens in the French style, and commissioned the Long Water, which, at a mile in length, almost but not quite rivalled Louis XIV's Grand Canal at Versailles.

This ostentatious French influence led to numerous formal gardens being created throughout England, most notably at Badminton House in Gloucestershire, Chatsworth in Derbyshire (see p.18), and Wrest Park in Bedfordshire (see p.42). Characterized by far-reaching vistas, broad avenues, parterres, fountains, and compartmentalized beds with embroidery-like designs and box edging, they were English exemplars of the French style.

Going Dutch

After the Glorious Revolution of 1688, co-rulers William III and Mary II brought a fresh flavour to Hampton Court from the Netherlands, having created their own Baroque gardens at their palace of Het Loo. The Dutch style was far smaller in

scale and simpler than the French, though still ornate. The Long Water, network of avenues, and parterres remained, but new introductions included topiary, more canals, and bright flowers – tulips especially, but also exotics (a passion of Mary's) procured by the Dutch East India Company. With the Privy Garden and Great Maze also added by William and Mary, the gardens at Hampton Court were now arguably at their finest.

Many of the great Dutch-inspired gardens were landscaped over in the 18th century, but we do have illustrations that give an insight into their magnificence, as well as some rare survivals in Gloucestershire. Remnants of a Dutch water garden are still visible at Dyrham Park, while a fine restored example at Westbury Court Garden, with its banqueting pavilion and canal lined with topiary-topped yew hedging, gives a far better impression of how these gardens once looked.

The English Renaissance

The ultimate influence in England during this period, however, came from Italian Renaissance gardens – the foundation of both the French and Dutch interpretations. Inspired by ancient Greek and Roman ideas and the Mediterranean climate, Italian Renaissance gardens were designed as open-air rooms, employing architectural features such as geometric layouts, terraces, shaded pergolas, pavilions, grottos, classical sculpture, clipped evergreens, and

water features. The 16th-century creations at Villa d'Este in Tivoli, Villa Lante in Bagnaia, and Boboli Gardens in Florence were legendary throughout Europe.

This fundamental design style spread to Tudor England during the reign of Henry VIII – a self-styled Renaissance man – and matured in the early 1600s, with important (and now lost) examples at Wilton House near Salisbury and Moor Park in Hertfordshire. It has endured to the present day (see The Laskett, p.36), ensuring the ongoing influence of Italy and the formal style throughout the development of England's gardens.

A plan of the gardens at Wilton House, one of the first parterre gardens in England, established by French landscape architect Isaac de Caus in 1632

Chatsworth

A glorious garden that melds European influences, English landscape design, and Victorian engineering.

Chatsworth House with its vast Canal Pond and Emperor Fountain, set amid 1,000 acres of landscaped parkland

The first glimpses of Chatsworth, near Bakewell in Derbyshire, are unforgettable. On a bright morning, the house dazzles, majestic in its Derwent Valley setting with wooded hills behind. All you can see is owned by the estate, and the views are extensive indeed.

Fashionably formal

Chatsworth has belonged to the Cavendish family since 1549. Elizabeth Talbot, Countess of Shrewsbury – better known as Bess of Hardwick – and her second husband, William Cavendish (1st Earl of Devonshire), built the first house on the site, with a modest formal garden. By the late 17th century, it was in need of repair. Eager to match his home to his status, William Cavendish, 4th Earl of Devonshire (and later 1st Duke), rebuilt the house in phases from 1687 to 1707. A fashionable residence required a fashionable setting, so the earl commissioned high-society favourites George London and Henry Wise (see p.24) to create a sloped parterre garden. Inspired by French, Italian, and Dutch formal gardens, it was decorated with sculptures and water features, including the Seahorse Fountain, positioned centrally on what is now the South Lawn and fed from a pipe at the base of the stepped Cascade.

Fashionably natural

William Cavendish, 4th Duke of Devonshire, next made his mark on the grounds, creating the approach from the west that today renders even the most loquacious visitor speechless. He also removed part of Edensor village to ensure uninterrupted views from Chatsworth House. By the time landscape designer Lancelot "Capability" Brown arrived in 1758, the formal gardens had been levelled and

grassed over, most of the large fountains taken out, and the topiary and formal avenues removed. Brown added a ha-ha (a sunken wall), creating a seamless transition between garden and park. In pursuit of "natural" beauty, he planted trees throughout the park and even altered the course of the River Derwent.

The 4th Duke's garden is largely the one we see today, with 19th-century additions by the 6th Duke, William Spencer Cavendish, and his head gardener, engineering genius Joseph Paxton, who trained at the Horticultural Society's experimental gardens in Chiswick. Paxton created Victorian parterre gardens, along with a majestic conservatory to house the duke's extensive exotic plant collection. The forerunner of London's Crystal Palace, which Paxton also designed, Chatsworth's Great Conservatory was demolished in 1920, and the remaining walls now house the Maze.

Paxton went on to design the alpine Rock Garden, as well as the iconic Emperor Fountain, whose powerful jet is recorded to have reached 90 m (295 ft) high. One of horticulture's unsung heroes, Sarah Paxton took on many of the head gardener's duties in her husband's absence, using her extensive plant knowledge and engineering education to manage Chatsworth's exotic planting and oversee construction projects.

Historically and horticulturally, Chatsworth is one of the most significant properties in England. It is also immaculately maintained and staggeringly beautiful. Yet it continues to develop: contemporary additions include naturalistic designer Dan Pearson's RHS Chelsea Flower Show 2015 winner, the Chatsworth Laurent-Perrier Garden, and landscape architect Tom Stuart-Smith's superb new planting in the Rockery, Arcadia, and Maze Garden.

above *Designed by Denis Fisher in 1962, the Maze is made up of more than 1,000 English yews;* **right** *Making repairs to the Great Conservatory at Chatsworth, in the late 19th century*

Chatsworth's grand, stepped Cascade was remodelled in 1708, after an earlier design by French engineer Monsieur Grillet in 1696. The new Cascade is much wider than the original and almost twice the length.

English formal Baroque

"... no one can be better furnish'd than they may by their Majesties Gard'ner and Mr. Wise... "

Thomas Langford, Plain and Full Instructions to Raise All Sorts of Fruit-Trees, *1696*

In the late 17th and early 18th centuries, an English version of the formal Baroque garden first developed in the grand palaces and houses of Europe. Due to the vast fortunes being made from expanding colonial trade, which profited hugely from the use of enslaved people on the plantations (see p.60), this was an era that saw a boom in country estate building – and country estates needed gardens. Garden designer George London and his apprentice and later business partner Henry Wise were the most influential nurserymen and garden makers of this era, specializing in this emergent style and enjoying a near monopoly on the larger landscape projects of the time.

Brompton Park Nursery

In 1681, George London became one of the co-founders of the acclaimed Brompton Park Nursery; then, in 1689, when the other founders had either died or retired, he was joined by his apprentice, the successful gardener Henry Wise. The pair would continue as sole partners until London's death in 1714, and under their auspices the nursery rapidly became one of the most successful of its day, largely thanks to their forwardthinking, but also the nursery's sheer size – the 100-acre site spanned the area of Kensington now covered by the Natural History Museum and the Victoria and Albert Museum, and stretching towards Knightsbridge.

This was a fertile area with good soil that had been utilized by numerous nurseries of differing sizes and specialities. However, the Brompton Park Nursery soon overshadowed all competition, establishing itself as the leading provider

The Great Garden at Hanbury Hall in Worcestershire, restored to its original English Baroque plan designed by George London and Henry Wise

of garden designs, fine plants, particularly mature topiary, hedging, and specimen trees. They amply served elite garden owners both in London and across the country from their well-stocked site. It is estimated that at its peak the nursery held approximately 10 million plants!

The London style

Though he had designed the great formal gardens at Blenheim Palace, Henry Wise was often referred to as the businessman of the two, while George London was considered the greater creative mind. The popularity of London's designs came from his understanding of the fashionable formal gardens of Europe, particularly the Dutch and French, noted for their intricate parterres reflecting the patterns of lace and broderie, their extensive use of topiary, their beautifully engineered water features, and their long tree-lined avenues or *allées*. In around 1700 George London journeyed to France to study the gardens there, and he came back inspired. He was particularly interested in the work of landscape architect André Le Nôtre, who had recently created the magnificent gardens at Versailles for Louis XIV, of which the whole of Europe was envious. However, London was no simple follower of fashion; he was also very aware of the writings of diarist and gardener John Evelyn, who advocated a softer, more naturalistic feel to gardens, with less regimented planting and views out to the wider countryside. London's designs merged both influences, often including a "Labyrinth or Grove" with surprisingly informal tree planting, captured within a formal layout of hedges and shady walks for maximum variety and interest.

This approach made London an early exponent of the naturalistic style that would later be associated more with William Kent and Lancelot "Capability" Brown, positioning him in the significant period of gradual transition from the formality of the Baroque style towards the more naturalized "English Landscape". London

The English Baroque gardens of Hampton Court Palace, depicted by Leonard Knyff in c. 1702–1704

gave an Englishness to the European style, which could be seen at some of his greatest commissions: Chatsworth (see p.18), Burghley House in Lincolnshire, Castle Howard in Yorkshire, and his final, and reputedly finest, landscape at the now-demolished Wanstead House in London. It made him a much-in-demand designer for the aspirational new estate owner.

Sadly, none of the gardens created by London and Wise survived the advent of the English Landscape Movement, though this may have been due just as much to the high costs of maintaining a formal garden as it was to changing fashions. However, glimpses of their style can still be seen, most notably at Melbourne Hall in Derbyshire, where the gardens have changed very little since the early 18th century when London and Wise helped create them. Elsewhere their designs have been lovingly reconstructed from the original plans: the Great Garden at Hanbury Hall near Worcester and the Privy Garden at Hampton Court Palace, with their contrasting geometric patterns,

regimented topiary, occasional serpentine lines, and surprising vistas, at least give us a small insight into the work of this hugely significant design duo.

Kip and Knyff

Painter Leonard Knyff and engraver Johannes Kip were the masters of creating bird's-eye views of most of the great English estates from the late 17th and early 18th centuries, usually commissioned by the owners to publicize their wealth and status, and impress their fellow landowners. The partnership between the two Dutchmen was significant in providing reliable illustrations of the development of the formal English garden in the Baroque style, capturing the great and largely lost era of the professional gardener – men (and it was only men at this stage) such as George London and Henry Wise, Charles Bridgeman, and Batty Langley, who were designers, but also engineers, earth movers, and plantsmen. Continuing a tradition begun by landscape painters such as Jan Siberechts and

> " The most valuable Labyrinths are always those that wind most, as that of Versailles, the Contrivance of which has been wonderfully lik'd by all that have seen it. "

London and Wise, The Retir'd Gardner, *1706*

Hendrik Danckerts earlier in the 17th century, Kip and Knyff perfected the style of the architectural print, seamlessly blending art and topography. Their illustrations, which were a cross between a landscape view and a map, are celebrated for their surprising detail, preserved in a series of plates that were expertly and imaginatively drawn by Knyff and engraved by Kip. The pair's most famous work, *Britannia Illustrata* – the first volume of which was published in 1707 – is among the most important English topographical publications of the 18th century. The architecture it depicts from on high, including royal palaces as well as fine country estates, is rendered in microscopic detail, with formal parterres and radiating avenues, *allées* and extended walkways driven through woods, and planting stretching out to the horizon, as well as statuary, gates, and other garden features, all etched out in fine black strokes.

These aerial views are also beautifully and often humorously staffed with active figures, coaches and horses, water craft on the rivers, and the delightful bustle of general life upon a well-mannered country estate. And all this conceived long before hot-air balloon ascension, let alone a drone! The two volumes of *Britannia Illustrata* compiled images of the very finest country estates of the era, preserving the past glories of many that are now irrevocably changed or indeed entirely lost to us, such as Cassiobury Park, one of the most significant landscapes in England, which is now a public park in Watford following the demolition of the house in 1927, and the lost formal gardens of Cassey Compton near Cheltenham and the ruined Hailes Abbey in the Cotswolds.

Sources of study

Kip and Knyff's engravings had until recently been dismissed as works of the imagination, designed to flatter their rich patrons. However, they are now being recognized as largely accurate and therefore immensely valuable in understanding the fashions, trends, and influences of the designed landscapes of this period. Within less than a generation the controlled formal gardens these illustrations document would be slowly and steadily transformed into the "naturalistic" compositions of the English Landscape Movement; therefore, the work of Kip and Knyff provides one of the most precious records we have of a style that is now sadly lost to time.

Longleat

Best known for its wildlife park, Longleat is one of the finest Elizabethan buildings in England, and its grounds tell the story of English garden design.

When you think of Longleat, lions and an eccentric marquess may be the first things that spring to mind. But the house, near Warminster in Wiltshire, is exquisite, and its gardens bear the mark of horticultural trends from the 17th century to the present day.

Built by John Thynne between 1568 and 1580, Longleat is an Elizabethan "prodigy house" – an ostentatious residence designed to impress royalty. The grounds were transformed a century later, when Thomas Thynne, 1st Viscount Weymouth, commissioned garden designer George London and the Brompton Park Nursery to conjure up a fashionably formal setting. The result was a Baroque masterpiece, resplendent with parterres, statues, fountains, a maze, and a canal. Tree-lined avenues extended towards the distant farmland, and a star of avenues cut through a woodland wilderness known as The Grove.

Pleasure grounds

In the 1730s, the hunt-loving 2nd Viscount, Thomas Thynne, gave the gardens a flamboyant, Rococo-style makeover (see p.74), complete with a menagerie of exotic animals. He softened London's Great Canal, giving it a serpentine shape, and planted more trees.

What remained of the formal structure was erased by Lancelot "Capability" Brown, who was employed between 1757 and 1762 by Thomas Thynne, 3rd Viscount Weymouth (later, 1st Marquess of Bath), to create a "natural" landscape. This is largely what we see today: sweeping lawns planted with clumps of trees, the enlarged serpentine river, and beautifully considered lakes. Brown extended the view across the landscape by installing a ha-ha, (a sunken wall to contain livestock) improved the

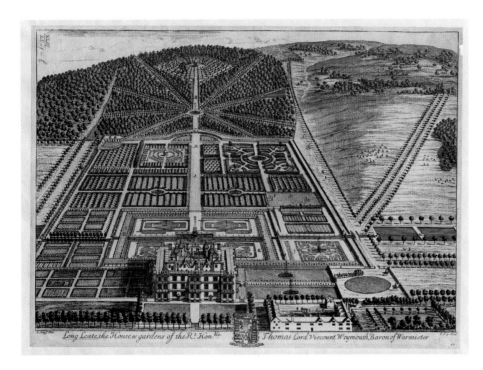

Long Leate, the House & gardens of the R.t Hon.ble Thomas Lord Viscount Weymouth, Baron of Warminster

left *Kip and Knyff's plan of the original gardens at Longleat, 1707;* **below** *Jan Siberechts'* View of Longleat, *1678*

approach to the house with the new South Drive, and designed the Pleasure Walk arboretum, enticing visitors into the wider park to enjoy its spectacular views.

By the late 1780s, around 50,000 trees were being planted annually across the park and newly purchased moorland. The 3rd Viscount also created a large fishing lake, Shear Water, to which his successor added a Gothic boathouse and bridge (whose design featured in landscape gardener Humphry Repton's plans for Longleat).

Hedges and hippos

The 19th century saw a return to formality, with a series of geometric gardens to the east and north of the house, and ornamental planting along the Longcombe Drive approach. These were later simplified by garden designer Russell Page, working for the 5th and 6th marquesses. It was the latter, Henry Thynne, who sold off large portions of the estate to pay crippling death duties. In 1966, he opened Longleat Safari Park – and Lancelot "Capability" Brown's Half-Mile Lake was soon home to hippos!

Longleat's future was secure, but the story does not end here. Alexander Thynn, 7th Marquess of Bath – notorious for his many "wifelets" and unusual artistic tastes – added a selection of formal mazes and labyrinths, including the endless Hedge Maze.

For centuries, the gardens at Longleat have flipped from formal to informal and back again, but they have always been at the forefront of landscape design. The estate is now in the hands of Ceawlin Thynn, 8th Marquess of Bath, and the pattern looks set to continue – demonstrating how great English estates are entirely at the mercy of their owners.

above *Longleat's formal topiary and statuary, inspired by the Italian Renaissance style*

GENERAL VIEW OF LONGLEATE FROM THE PROSPECT HILL:
SHEWING THE WATER AS IT HAS BEEN FINISHED, AND THE SURFACE LOWERED, TO RAISE THE HOUSE.

Published by J Taylor, Feb 1 1816

left *Longleat House and grounds as seen from the Prospect Hill, by landscape designer Humphry Repton, 1816;* **below** *The Sun Maze and Lunar Labyrinth at Longleat today*

Formality
and
its
features

"Everything is protected by an enclosure... hidden and withdrawn from sight by the tiers of box..."

Pliny the Younger, Epistle v.6, to Apollinaris, c. 100 CE

The formal style that came to define the grand gardens of the 17th century had numerous characteristic elements that were almost a checklist of must-have features. Gardens at this time were designed to symbolize man's supremacy over the elements, and so the formal style required the sculpting hand of man to be evident. There was nothing wild or untamed in these gardens; geometry, symmetry, and pattern were the primary aesthetic principles, aimed at enhancing the beauty of nature with the guiding rules of artifice. The results suggested harmony, grandeur, wealth, power, order, control, stability – everything that the ruling classes wished to project.

The formal elements

Despite the variations of each particular formal style – Italian, French, or Dutch – the main elements of the English versions were surprisingly consistent. A unity of design extending from the main house was the ideal, and so the basic framework consisted of a geometric layout, with avenues of varying scales radiating from a central point (known as a *patte d'oie* or goose's foot). Parterre gardens, which had evolved from Tudor knot gardens, were an essential, usually intricately patterned, feature, created with clipped hedging in the European style, or with lawn, which was well suited to the British climate.

Water features – usually formal canals and ornate fountains – would animate the

layout and provide a sense of tranquillity, while aviaries were another common feature that would appeal to the senses. Statues, urns, and vases emphasized the owner's classical sensibilities, harking back to the elegance and artistic ideals of ancient Rome, while regimented, neatly shaped topiary represented the greatest expression of man's dominance over nature.

England's finest formal gardens

One of the most magnificent examples of the English formal garden was created at Badminton House in Gloucestershire, by Henry, 1st Duke of Beaufort, and his wife Mary – a keen and knowledgeable gardener – in the late 17th century. The garden comprised a resplendent series of radial avenues (the central one being almost 4 km/2.5 miles long!), a fantastic succession of parterre gardens, a bowling green, and bosquets (a formal plantation of trees), plus topiary, fountains, and terraces. As with so many formal gardens of the period, however, it was swept away by later alterations.

A better-preserved example is Melbourne Hall in Derbyshire, laid out by Sir Thomas Coke, Vice Chamberlain to Queen Anne, with help from George London and Henry Wise (see p.24), between 1704 and 1711. The vast gardens, with their parterres, radial avenues, lead statuary, fountains, and French-style wrought-iron arbour, have undergone few major alterations since. Others may not be original but live on in spirit. The majestic parterre created at Kirby Hall in Northamptonshire by Sir Christopher Hatton III in the 1690s – once fully enclosed in a stone wall and entered by a magnificent gateway – did not survive the 18th century but has since been reconstructed with an intricate gravel-and-grass cutwork design.

So it was that English aristocrats sought to make their mark on the land they conspicuously owned, with numerous grand houses following suit. The formal garden would become a repeating theme in garden design right up to today, and although the scale would alter over time, the fundamental elements remained.

A 17th-century painting of a formal garden, with fountains, swans, and topiary, which hangs at Packwood House, Warwickshire

Topiary

An essential element of all great formal gardens, topiary is the art of pruning shrubs and trees into ornamental shapes. Its popularity has ebbed and flowed over the centuries, but with each revival, topiary has been used in different ways to suit an ever-wider range of gardens.

As with so many gardening techniques, topiary can be traced back to Italy. In his encyclopaedic work *Historia Naturalis* (*c*.77 CE), Roman scholar Pliny the Elder credited Gaius Matius Calvinus with introducing topiary to Roman gardens, while his nephew, Pliny the Younger, later described in a letter the magnificent gardens at his own villa, with their "sloping ridge with figures of animals on both sides cut out of the box-trees", and "a walk bordered by evergreens pressed and trimmed into various shapes".

The royal influence

Throughout history, topiary has fallen in and out of favour, largely due to the expense of maintaining it. Its first revival came in the 16th century, when topiary became an essential element of the European elites' parterre gardens. At the same time, rural smallholders adopted this style for their burgeoning cottage gardens, as described by English pastoral poet Barnabe Googe in *Foure Bookes of Husbandrie* (1577), which talks of women clipping rosemary "as in the fashion of a cart, a peacock, or such things as they fancy".

It was the royals of the 17th century, however, who truly popularized the style, under the influence of Louis XIV's Palace of Versailles. Charles II lacked the funds to emulate the French king's flamboyant statement, so instead he adopted several design devices from Versailles – including wide avenues of clipped and framed box – and re-created them at Hampton Court Palace. It fell to William III and Mary II to invest in large-scale landscape designs, modelled on the more restrained Dutch planting style they had implemented at their palace at Het Loo in the Netherlands. William designed Hampton Court's new Privy Garden (beautifully restored in 1995) and also commissioned its hornbeam-hedged maze.

Where the royal family led, others were quick to follow, and topiary was soon introduced as a major design element in the gardens of many grand English houses. Levens Hall in Cumbria boasts the oldest original example in the world, with a wonderland of shapes dating from the 1690s. Topiary can also be found at Chastleton House in Oxfordshire, Dyrham

Park in Gloucestershire, Ham House in London, and Packwood House in Warwickshire – not to mention the magnificent Westbury Court Garden in Gloucestershire, one of the few surviving 17th-century Dutch-style gardens in the country. At this time, yew was the topiary plant of choice. Buxus (box) was avoided, condemned by Richard Surfleet in *Countrie Farm* (1600) as "of naughtie smell", and said to kill bees and "corrupteth the aire".

Changing fashions

Following the 17th-century heyday of the great formal garden, Enlightenment poet Alexander Pope dismissed topiary as a mere fashion in 1713, when he mocked the art in his essay *Verdant Sculpture*.

Meanwhile, the early 18th-century creators of the English landscape garden, including Charles Bridgeman, William Kent, and Lancelot "Capability" Brown, began to sweep the gardens of English nobles clean of hedges, mazes, and topiary. But although topiary fell from favour in elite circles, it remained a prized feature of cottage gardens, where a single example of a traditional form such as a ball or a tree trimmed to a cone, meticulously clipped and perhaps topped with a topiary peacock, took centre stage.

Following further revivals in the 19th century and during the Arts and Crafts Movement (see p.102), and no longer the preserve of the large formal garden, topiary continues to be popular today. It can be seen in the work of British garden designer Arne Maynard and Dutch plantsman Piet Oudolf, whose naturalistic planting at Scampston Hall in North Yorkshire (see p.162) contrasts beautifully with the tightly clipped forms of the topiary, while the garden of Charlotte and Donald Molesworth in Benenden, Kent (see p.177), is filled with an overwhelming array of sculpted shapes – a clear endorsement of the fact that topiary never goes out of fashion for long.

JAMES SHIRLEY HIBBERD

1825–1890

Successive generations of horticulturalists would rediscover the charm of topiary, among them James Shirley Hibberd, a climate activist, vegetarian, and true Renaissance man in Victorian garden circles. Dubbed the "father of amateur gardening", Hibberd was a champion of gardening devices that suited the burgeoning amateur suburban garden. He recognized the significance of the English cottage garden as a style, and advocated the use of topiary. In this he apparently disagreed with his outspoken contemporary, the Irish gardener and writer William Robinson, who rejected all forms of pruning and shaping.

The Laskett

A theatrical 20th-century spin on the early English formal garden, which pays faithful tribute to the design features of the Italian Renaissance.

Few gardens could be more personal than the Laskett, beautifully situated near the River Wye on the Welsh border. It is a stage set of a garden that celebrates the lives and work of its creators, Roy Strong, former director of London's National Portrait Gallery and the Victoria and Albert Museum, and his wife, renowned theatre set designer Julia Trevelyan Oman.

The couple moved to Herefordshire in 1973 and began work on their garden the following year. Flamboyant, unashamedly autobiographical, and not to everyone's taste, the Laskett uses a clever concoction of formal elements, including hedges, sculptures, and topiary, to guide the visitor through the garden. Every trick known to garden designers is used, from deep hedging backed by pleached limes to eye-catchers and defined views through hedges – all of which make the garden seem far larger than its four acres.

The Laskett's many classical touches, inspired by the Renaissance so adored by Roy, are carefully choreographed. Theatrical references to Julia's work also abound, among them the Ashton Arbour (a tribute to Covent Garden choreographer Frederick Ashton) and the *Die Fledermaus* Walk (named after her production of the operetta), which ends with a pinnacle bearing the Oman family coat of arms.

Curtain up

The performance begins at the front of the house with the Fountain Court, then continues along the main avenue to the Colonnade, an outdoor theatre that occupies the space of the former kitchen garden (Julia's domain until her death in 2003). Further avenues lead to other gardens, each with personal touches. At one end of the Elizabeth Tudor Walk – a scaled-up version of the Lime Walk at Sissinghurst – is the Shakespeare Monument, which commemorates the prize Roy won in 1980 for his contribution to the arts. Another avenue, Tatiana's Walk, concludes with a huge stag on a plinth bearing text from English poet John Milton's epic *Paradise Lost*. And at the heart of the Silver Jubilee Garden is a sundial from the Wiltshire garden of Roy's friend Cecil Beaton, the photographer famed for his royal portraits.

The garden's strong architectural form continues to the rear of the house, with the formal Yew Garden, designed by Julia, and the Nymphaeum, a Roman-style grotto built in 2015 to mark Roy's 80th birthday. Another recent classical addition is the Belvedere. This pavilion offers an elevated view of the garden – a must-have in 17th-century garden design. The vistas are enhanced by an impressive audio system, through which Roy explains what you are seeing at each point in the garden, and what it represents. This heightened sensory experience is a nod to the picturesque 18th-century gardens of the Wye Valley, where poems were strategically placed in beautiful spots.

The Laskett is a lesson in all that is classical in garden history. The sheer concentration of trickery, sculptures, topiary, and views make it a masterclass in design – one that continues to evolve in the hands of its new owners, the horticulture charity Perennial. In Roy's words: "A garden is an ever-evolving creation – like a painting that is never finished."

left *The topiary and classical statues are just some of the Laskett's many Renaissance-inspired features*

Travels and journeys

"Mere picturesque improvement is not enough in these enlightened times."

John Claudius Loudon, Gardener's Magazine, *1832*

Today garden visiting is a major pastime across the social spectrum, but centuries ago it was the exclusive privilege of the landed gentry. With few good roads and only horse and carriage for transportation, travel in England was arduous, tiresome, and expensive. Intrepid travellers were few, and even rarer were those who wrote up what they saw.

Celia Fiennes

One remarkable exception was Celia Fiennes, ancestor of the present Fiennes dynasty, who in the late 1600s started exploring every county of England riding side-saddle on horseback, often alone except for two servants – an extraordinary undertaking at that time, especially for a single woman. Trekking along roads that were barely clay tracks, through a landscape that was mostly still unenclosed wilderness, Fiennes made several journeys, mostly between 1685 and 1702. Upon her return to the family seat at Broughton Castle in Oxfordshire, she wrote an account of her travels that remained unpublished until long after her death.

Fiennes provided vivid descriptions of her many points of fascination: the emergent fashionable spa towns, the "production and manufactures of each place", the terrain and agricultural uses of the surrounding land. But her privileged access to England's aristocratic homes offers a valuable first-hand account of some of the finest gardens (sometimes still under construction) being created at this significant time, which often, together with Kip and Knyff's illustrations (see p.26), prove an invaluable source in the study of garden history. At Chatsworth,

(see p.18) she saw formal gardens with "stone statues in them" and fountains at their centre – all since lost to centuries of re-landscaping – as well as a large fountain full of "sea gods and dolphins and sea horses", which can still be seen today.

Garden tourism

Fiennes had anticipated by centuries what is often regarded as a post-Second World War phenomenon, and in the early 18th century some landowners were beginning to recognize the potential of opening their estates to the wider fee-paying public, with Stowe (see p.62) being one of the first in 1724 (though there were reports of vetting at the gatehouse to assess visitors' suitability). By 1774, that leader of fashion Horace Walpole was selling tickets for his fantasy Gothic castle Strawberry Hill – though only to four tourists a day.

By the 19th century, a new affluent middle class created by the Industrial Revolution was seeking to escape the slag heaps and smoke in favour of an earlier romantic vision of "Old England", while reformers such as John Claudius Loudon – botanist, garden designer, and author – heralded the democratization of gardens by revolutionizing public spaces and sharing his knowledge and ideas. He did this in works such as *In Search of English Gardens*, which surveyed the great gardens during the 1830s and 1840s, and his pioneering *Gardener's Magazine*.

Come the 20th century, following two world wars and the breakdown of the British Empire, society was changing. The rapid growth of the railways and car manufacturing led tourists out of the cities, and with a needy eye upon increasing taxes and running costs, estate owners welcomed them tentatively. The National Trust had been founded in 1895, but the first of the privately owned houses to break ranks was Longleat (see p. 28) in 1949, rapidly followed by Beaulieu and Woburn Abbey. The money-making potential was obvious, and with demolition sometimes the only alternative, many more followed.

The South Front of Horace Walpole's Twickenham estate Strawberry Hill, 18th century. Walpole saw the commercial benefits of garden tourism early, opening his house to the public in 1774

Taste makers

> "Delightful scenes ... have a kindly influence on the body, as well as the mind."
>
> *Joseph Addison,* The Spectator, *1712*

Taste in gardens during the late 17th century was dominated by the French desire for formality and strict symmetry, as seen at the masterpiece of the Palace of Versailles. However, at the dawning of the 18th century huge changes were beginning to happen culturally: as the Age of Enlightenment gathered pace, revolutionary ideas in art, philosophy, and science filtered through to country house architecture and their gardens. The Baroque was being replaced by classically inspired Palladian architecture set within sweeping lawns, wide vistas, and naturalistic woodlands, and the English upper classes, made wealthy by an empire built on slavery, were keen to make or remodel their country estates in this new home-grown style: the English Landscape Movement.

It has often been said that the movement was inspired by the returning Grand Tourists (see p.48) and their newly acquired landscape paintings by French Baroque artists Claude Lorrain and Nicolas Poussin, but that was not the only cause. Politics and economics also played a part, as did some of the key authors and poets of the age.

A new style

The charge began in 1712 when writer and Whig politician Joseph Addison wrote an essay for *The Spectator*, in which he railed against the formal garden, and particularly topiary. Addison argued instead for a more naturalistic approach – a "pretty landskip" – and the idea appealed to country house

Jacob with Laban and his Daughters, 1676, by Claude Lorrain, one of several Baroque painters whose classically inspired landscapes greatly influenced the look of the English Landscape Movement

owners, not just for aesthetic reasons, but pragmatic ones, too: a formal Baroque garden was an expensive thing to maintain, while the planting of new woodlands would add further benefits as the country was always in need of timber for shipping. Addison also made the connection between liberty in politics and liberty in landscape, which he believed would appeal to the Whig tendencies of the landed gentry.

Alexander Pope, meanwhile, argued in his poetry that the perfect garden should, in the Augustan style, surprise, delight, and strike a balance between nature and artifice. This was the advice he offered his great friends Henrietta Howard, Countess of Suffolk, as she began building a villa at Twickenham in 1723, which we now know as Marble Hill, and Richard Boyle, Earl of Burlington, when he started creating his house and garden at Chiswick in 1725 with designer William Kent – now regarded as the birthplace of the English Landscape Movement.

Influential, too, were the artist William Hogarth's theories on what constituted aesthetic beauty. In his 1753 book *The Analysis of Beauty*, he discussed the power and elegance of the serpentine line, particularly when used sparingly within a landscape. This idea presented a very different definition of beauty to the French ideal, which saw mathematics and geometry as its purist form, and it was readily taken up by William Kent and other landscape architects who were spearheading the movement.

This new wave of thought would lead to the creation of the natural pastoral landscapes that came to characterize the English Landscape Movement, shifting garden design slowly but surely from the rigid geometry of Baroque formalism to the sweeping lawns of Arcadian classicism, and creating a new style that, despite the obvious classical references, was regarded as wholly English.

CHARLES BRIDGEMAN
1690–1738

Charles Bridgeman is one of the most significant yet unsung figures in the transition of English landscape design from the formal to the naturalistic, having been overshadowed by his better-known successors, William Kent and Lancelot "Capability" Brown. Bridgeman began as an apprentice to Henry Wise at the Brompton Park Nursery (see p.24).

His great opportunity would come in 1711 when he began work at Stowe (see p.62) for Richard Temple, 1st Viscount Cobham, on an extravagant, indeed monumental, design that would include temples, an Egyptian pyramid, pillars, majestic avenues, summerhouses, formal canals – and the country's first ever "ha-ha" (a sunken wall). Bridgeman would go on to work at the most recognized estate landscapes in England, including Cassiobury Park and Claremont.

CASE STUDY

Wrest Park

This chateau-style house and its extensive 18th-century formal pleasure grounds, enclosed by canals, exude French splendour.

Wrest Park, near Silsoe in Bedfordshire, is the ultimate formal garden. Designed (most likely) by Baroque garden specialists George London and Henry Wise (see p.24) in the early 18th century, with subtle later alterations by Lancelot "Capability" Brown, these magnificent pleasure grounds remain largely intact due to the efforts of Jemima, Marchioness Grey, and her daughter Amabel.

Inspired by the extravagant formal gardens of Europe, the oldest surviving parts of Wrest Park's gardens include the Long Water canal – the central element of the 18th-century garden laid out for Henry Grey, 1st Duke of Kent. Architect Thomas Archer's fine Baroque pavilion (a banqueting hall) sits at the end of the Long Water, with designer Batty Langley's formal woodland garden on either side, dotted with sculptures, ornaments, and other garden buildings.

Set piece

In 1740, Jemima, Marchioness Grey, inherited Wrest Park. Tutored in landscape design and architecture by polymath Thomas Wright, she had a clear vision for the grounds. As well as maintaining the existing gardens, Jemima added her own touches. Her Chinois tableau, reminiscent of Chinese porcelain patterns, includes a wooden Chinese bridge, a temple, and a conch-shell water feature, interplanted with willow, acer, and tulip trees, and was highly fashionable (see p.72). She also added the Bath House, a rustic thatched folly with a floor of cobbles and deer antlers, built between 1769 and 1771 by architect Edward Stevens.

Jemima employed Lancelot "Capability" Brown to alter the landscape surrounding the formal gardens, and to naturalize the canals adjoining the Long Water. She kept a watchful eye on the landscape

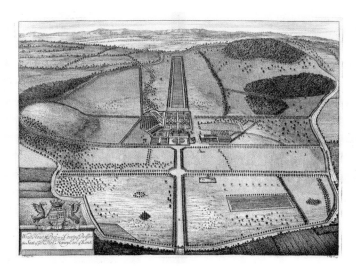

left *Engraving of Wrest Park by Johannes Kip and Leonard Knyff, 1709;* **below** *A wide path leads to the Long Water, created in the early 1680s, and the Archer Pavilion beyond, completed in 1711*

*The formal parterre garden at Wrest Park, complete
with classical statues, is an early 18th-century survivor,
possibly laid out by George London and Henry Wise*

above Portrait of the Ladies Amabel and Mary Jemima Yorke, *c. 1761, by Sir Joshua Reynolds. The girls are depicted in the grounds of Wrest Park. Their mother, Jemima, was a dominant force in the garden's redesign in the mid 1700s*

designer, ensuring that his amendments were restrained. The column she erected in 1770, engraved with thanks for "the professional assistance of Lancelot Brown Esq", raises the question of whether she was trying to conceal her own changes to the landscape, or whether – since his involvement was minimal – the inscription was tongue-in-cheek.

Fit for an empress

Such was the success of Jemima's alterations that, in 1774, her daughter Amabel was asked to sketch the gardens for inclusion in Wedgwood's "Frog Service", a vast dinner service made for Catherine the Great, Empress of Russia. Amabel inherited Wrest in 1797, but her expenditure was curtailed by the economic backlash of the Anglo-Spanish War, the French Revolution, and land enclosure. She made few changes to the gardens, but kept them in good order while repairing the house – even melting down sculptures to produce lead for the roof.

Despite Amabel's efforts, the house was demolished by her successor, Thomas Robinson, 2nd Earl de Grey. An amateur architect, he designed the new Wrest House in the style of an 18th-century French chateau, complete with stables, orangery, kitchen garden, and lodges. By repositioning the house further north, he was able to extend, rather than redo, the grounds, adding formal flower gardens and French-style parterre planting.

Wrest Park is a survivor – a rare example of the grand formal style. Although the estate fell into decline and was sold after the First World War, its stunning house and gardens, now maintained by English Heritage, are well worth visiting.

beauty

and the

perfection

"Nature has chosen [green] for the vestment of the earth,
and with the beauty of which the eye never tires."

William Hogarth, The Analysis of Beauty, *1753*

# of nature

The Grand Tour

"One of the most picturesque
scenes in the world."

Horace Walpole, on Stourhead, in Journals of
Visits to Country Seats, *1762*

The phrase "the Grand Tour", coined in the late 17th century, refers to the wondrous journey through Europe that most rich young men undertook, to drink in the culture of classical antiquity and collect art, sculpture, and ideas. As such, the Grand Tour's influence on elite culture in Britain, particularly during the 18th and early 19th centuries, was immense.

A gentleman's education

As the Age of Enlightenment dawned, being wealthy alone was no longer sufficient; the landed gentry needed to be cultured and well educated as well, and to demonstrate their fine taste. And so they would embark on the Grand Tour as a rite of passage that would educate them in the arts (and, it must be said, in far more worldly pleasures, too).

The trend reached its peak between the 1760s and 1790s, and would continue into the 1840s. It was no easy adventure; travel in this era could be arduous, even treacherous, while political turmoil – notably the French Revolution and Napoleonic Wars – periodically made certain countries uninviting.

Ordinarily, however, Paris would be the first stop, where the young traveller would be polished in style and manners, then onwards, across the Alps – a particularly tough journey, as it involved being carried in a sedan chair along the mountain paths. Italy was essential, where tourists would visit all the great cities (Venice, Florence, Rome, and Naples), admiring the art, architecture, and churches, attending a masked ball or two, and maybe picking up the odd Canaletto or three. From Naples, some explored the excavations at Herculaneum and Pompeii; the more adventurous even ascended Mount Vesuvius, which was particularly active in the 1760s and 1770s.

Some explored the Ottoman Empire, while others ventured back across the Alps, through Switzerland, Austria, and Germany, perhaps with a period of study at the universities in Munich or Heidelberg. It's hardly surprising that most Grand Tours lasted for several years.

Grand souvenirs

Almost as important as the Tour itself were the mementos travellers brought back, which served as symbols of their status. The wealthiest Grand Tourists would return with crates full of books, art, scientific instruments, and cultural artefacts, ranging from snuff boxes and paperweights to religious altars, fountains, and statuary – all to be ostentatiously displayed at their country estates.

Particularly à la mode was a portrait of the Grand Tourist painted against a beautiful classical setting. Landscape artists too, such as French Baroque painter Claude Lorrain, were creating Arcadian scenes of ancient ruins and temples, which many travellers were inspired to emulate in their own grounds. Wealthy banker Henry Hoare II, for example, toured Italy from 1738 to 1741. When he returned to inherit Stourhead, in Wiltshire, he began transforming the gardens into a neo-classical landscape that many believe represents Aeneas's journey from Trojan war hero to the founder of Rome in Virgil's *Aeneid*, in direct reference to Lorrain's 1672 painting *Landscape with Aeneas at Delos*. Hoare knew fellow gentlemen travellers would appreciate the allusions.

The Grand Tourist's garden

Hoare was not the only one to try to re-create the classical world at home. Estate gardens were littered with the spoils of the master's adventures. In contrast to the formality that had long dominated English garden design, many returned from Italy with plans to create a new style that was far more naturalistic, inspired by the country's art and culture.

Influential men such as Richard Boyle, 3rd Earl of Burlington, and landscape architect William Kent spent years in Italy during the early 1700s. Entranced by the more "natural" elements of gardens such as the Renaissance Villa Lante in Bagnaia –

British Gentlemen in Rome, *painted by Scottish portrait artist, Katharine Read c.1750 shows well-to-do Grand Tourists beside the city's famous monuments* particularly the *bosco*, or woodland park, which, though contrived, still imitated nature – they realized the same ideas could be used at estates back home. The juxtaposition of nature and artifice, the idea of man working *with* nature, not subjugating it, appealed to the English sensibility and would become the basis of the new English landscape garden.

The Augustan fields

As England's Grand Tourists returned, their heads filled with the beauty, poetry, and politics of ancient Rome, they ushered in a new Augustan Age that would characterize the first half of the 18th century. In literature, it produced the likes of Alexander Pope and Joseph Addison (see p.41), who imitated Horace and Virgil, hoping to emulate their refinement and welcome a period of political power, high culture, and stability similar to the reign of Augustus. And in garden design,

it led to magnificent transformations, as the formal gardens of estates up and down the country were drastically remodelled in the new English Landscape style.

The pioneer architects of the movement – Charles Bridgeman, William Kent, and Lancelot "Capability" Brown – created renowned classical landscapes at estates such as Stowe (see p.62), with essential features including lakes, grottos, woodlands, sweeping lawns, and intriguing serpentine walks, plus obligatory Roman temples and sculpture. Castle Howard in Yorkshire embodied the philosophy. Despite its beginnings in 1699 as a Baroque confection of cherubs and coronets, the later additions of a Palladian wing and an Arcadian parkland make it a gem of the naturalistic Augustan style. Pastoral lakes, cascades, and woodland surround the house, while the Temple of the Four Winds and the domed Mausoleum, built in the 1720s, stand majestic at the far end of the park.

William Kent, however, who "saw that all nature was a garden" according to Horace Walpole, was perhaps the most influential architect of this Augustan period. His most successful and complete garden, Rousham in Oxfordshire (see p.52), remains one of the most outstanding in England, while Chiswick House in London, which he created with his great friend Richard Boyle, the Earl of Burlington, in 1725–1738, is considered the "birthplace" of the English Landscape Movement. Alexander Pope's epistle to

An 18th-century painting of the Italianate gardens at Chiswick House, designed by William Kent and Richard Boyle, who drew inspiration from their travels on the Grand Tour

Burlington, written in 1731 during the project, shows how the pair were putting the Augustan ideals of elegant simplicity into practice: "You show us, Rome was glorious, not profuse."

Copied abroad

The English Landscape Movement, with its idealized view of nature, was so popular it became a rare example of an English style that would go on to inspire many gardens in Europe, rather than the other way around. By the 1750s, tourists and writers were describing what they'd seen in England, and the ideas soon spread, replacing the French formal style that had dominated in the 17th century.

One of the first English-style gardens in Europe was at Ermenonville, in France, built by René Louis de Girardin, Marquis of Vauvray, from 1763 to 1776, which he based on the ideals of his tutor and hero Jean-Jacques Rousseau. The Swiss-born philosopher revered the image of a garden that reflected nature, and so, inspired by a visit to Stowe, Girardin created a garden at Ermenonville so naturalistic it seemed almost untouched by human hands – though it certainly had been touched by the 100 English gardeners he'd hired to create it. The marquis also built a romantic cottage for Rousseau in the park's wilderness, which so enchanted Rousseau that he lived, died, and was buried there.

Other English gardens sprang up across Europe in the second half of the 18th century, notably in France, Germany, Poland, and Russia. Even at Versailles – the original icon of the French formal style, which had inspired so many imitations – Marie-Antoinette added a small English landscape park with its own Corinthian monument and grotto. The cycle of influence between England and the Continent had, it seems, come full circle.

The gardens at Castle Howard, Yorkshire, combine elements of Augustan and Arcadian styles, along with formal topiary and the later addition of the 19th-century Atlas Fountain

CASE STUDY

Rousham

This masterpiece by William Kent is one of the most individual of English landscape gardens, and the most complete remaining example of his work.

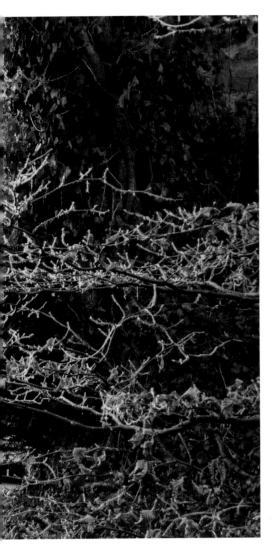

The seven-arch arcade (Praeneste), designed by William Kent and inspired by the architecture of ancient Rome

If ever a garden was having a renaissance of popularity, it would be Rousham, near Bicester in Oxfordshire. But it has always been a favourite of mine. At times this 18th-century garden seems almost modern, with its limited colour palette and naturalistic planting. The calm romanticism of its atmosphere and the intimacy of the landscape also add to its appeal.

The gardens at Rousham were first designed in the 1730s by Charles Bridgeman, whose burgeoning naturalistic style had become highly fashionable. As at Claremont (see p.56) and Stowe (see p.62), landscape architect William Kent (commissioned by General James Dormer, whose family still owns Rousham) then took up the mantle, altering and embellishing Bridgeman's framework and remodelling the 17th-century house. Bridgeman created meandering walks with a succession of formal pools; Kent transformed these into an Augustan landscape, recalling the atmosphere of ancient Rome with his perfectly positioned groves, streams, cascades, and classical architectural elements.

Mythical landscape

From the start, we are guided by the design. Looking across the immaculate bowling green, the eye is drawn to Belgian sculptor Peter Scheemakers' *A Lion Attacking a Horse*, and then – pausing to take in the verdant Oxfordshire countryside – to a triumphal arch in the distance.

The shadowy entrance to the garden is succeeded by the first of many open, light groves, where the *Dying Gladiator*, another Scheemakers sculpture, is positioned ponderously on a classical plinth. Statues of the immortal Pan and Hercules hint at moral

above *The octagonal cold bath and rill that meanders through the woodland are disarmingly modern-looking features;* **right** *The River Cherwell flows below the gardens, seen here from the grand Praeneste*

dilemmas. This is an interactive landscape, peopled with characters Kent discovered on his Grand Tour and employed to theatrical effect.

Kent's Venus Vale incorporates Bridgeman's formal pool and titillates with yet more statuary. Once again we move from darkness to light, enticed by a serpentine rill (a narrow channel of water) into a grove where the rill expands into a cold bath, with all the charged eroticism such sensationalist features are designed to prompt. This is a pleasure garden indeed!

Bucolic bliss

The pièce de résistance in this overwhelming sensory experience is the seven-arched Praeneste arcade, designed to present the broad view across the River Cherwell and the countryside below. Here, wooden benches hint at illicit liaisons as well as offering a chance to soak up the Arcadian atmosphere. Whatever its use, the Praeneste stands as testament to Kent's architectural genius.

Beyond Bridgeman's ha-ha, rare long-horned cattle dot the landscape near where a wooden bridge once crossed the river. Now, visitors climb back up the hill towards the house to experience the profuse colour of the 17th-century walled gardens – a dazzling treat for eyes grown used to green. An archway leads from one walled garden into the next – the kitchen garden – and from there into a third, where an elegant dovecote overlooks a box parterre.

Rousham is an intensely personal experience. It is also a masterful expression of restraint and a magical landscape with a narrative that few can emulate or even aspire to do so. Without question, this is one of England's most influential gardens, and it is certainly William Kent's finest.

Claremont Landscape Garden

This 18th-century haven not far from the capital is one of the earliest surviving examples of the naturalistic English landscape garden style.

Praised as "the noblest of any in Europe" by garden designer Stephen Switzer in 1726, Claremont Landscape Garden boasts work by some of the best-known landscape architects of the 18th century. Although the estate was designed for pleasure and respite from public life, several of its most famous occupants were unable to reap its benefits.

Architect John Vanbrugh built himself a modest country retreat near Esher, Surrey, in 1709. He sold the property five years later to Thomas Pelham-Holles, Duke of Newcastle (and later prime minister), but stayed to help develop the house and gardens. Vanbrugh's Belvedere Tower, positioned on a hill, was both a highly visible status symbol and, with a telescope installed on the roof, the perfect spot for stargazing and keeping an eye on the neighbours!

An English landscape garden

In the 1720s, the duke commissioned pioneering designer Charles Bridgeman to create a formal garden at Claremont. Bridgeman's legacy includes the iconic 3-acre turf amphitheatre, meticulously carved into what is now dubbed "Bridgeman's Hill". This unusual feature formed the centrepiece of the *fête champêtre*, an annual garden party in which hundreds of visitors were treated to music, theatre, and spectacular fireworks.

Claremont's formal garden was short-lived: by the 1730s, garden designers were favouring the more naturalistic approach. The duke brought in leading landscape architect William Kent to replant much of the garden in a "natural" style. Many of Bridgeman's features, including the amphitheatre and ha-ha, survived the transition, but Kent softened the formal round pond, giving it a serpentine shape and adding an island with a pavilion. This enabled the duke and

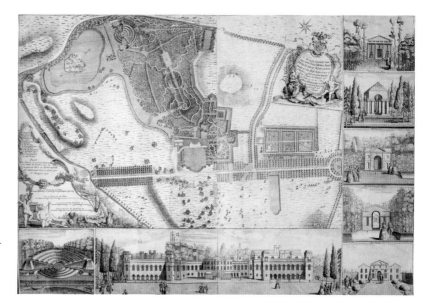

*right Plan of the park at Claremont by John Rocque, 1738; **below** Illustration of the South Front of Claremont by John Hassel, 1817, during the residence of Princess Charlotte*

SOUTH FRONT OF CLAREMONT

The Seat of Her Royal Highness Princess Charlotte of Saxe Cobourg

taken with her Royal Highnesses special permission by J. Hassell 1817.

right View from the top of the grass amphitheatre, designed by Charles Bridgeman; **below** The naturalistic 18th-century park, as remodelled by William Kent and Lancelot "Capability" Brown

duchess to indulge in boating on the lake, as well as hosting all manner of lavish entertainments.

The couple loved Claremont, but their extravagant lifestyle was unsustainable. Following the duke's death in 1768, the estate was sold to Robert Clive, known as Clive of India. Clive employed designer-of-choice Lancelot "Capability" Brown to relocate the obtrusive road and help build a grander mansion. Brown also altered the line of the ha-ha and planted the amphitheatre with evergreen trees and shrubs to hide what he denounced as a formal feature. Unfortunately, having spent around £100,000 remodelling the estate, Clive died before it was completed.

Royal refuge

Claremont later became a sanctuary for royalty: in the early 19th century Princess Charlotte (heir to the British throne) and Prince Leopold of Saxe-Coburg made it their brief but happy marital home. The couple added various features to the gardens, including a heated greenhouse – the base of which forms the current Camellia Terrace. Work began on Charlotte's elaborate neo-Gothic tea house in 1816, but when she died in 1817 following the birth of their stillborn son, Leopold reinvented the building as a memorial to his beloved wife.

The garden's 18th-century layout is still largely intact, and the National Trust has done much to restore Claremont to its former glory. The Duke of Newcastle's words from 1765 remain apt: "Dear Claremont was never in greater beauty. Everything green, the trees charmingly come out, the wood delightful."

Politics, economics, and empire

"All the world are mad about building
as far as they can reach."

*John Vanbrugh, writing on the British landed gentry,
in a letter to the Earl of Carlisle, 1721*

Many of England's most significant gardens are attached to the great stately homes scattered across the country, long prized as a quintessential part of our national heritage. These grand mansions hark back to an earlier age of ostentation and elegance. They are hugely popular visitor attractions for locals and tourists alike, not to mention the famous locations for films and TV shows from *Pride and Prejudice* to *Downton Abbey*.

So far, so glamorous. But there is a sinister side to these estates that must be acknowledged alongside their grandeur and cultural importance. Many of them were built as expressions of power and privilege, during a period of British imperial expansion, when trade and capitalism became the nation's driving force. This generated huge wealth and influence, produced great works of art and architecture, and powered the Industrial Revolution, but at its heart was based in terrible human exploitation.

Slavery and the English country house

In recent years, England's colonial past, and particularly its role in the Atlantic slave trade, has received greater public attention. When the National Trust commissioned a report in 2020, which found that at least 93 of the 300 houses in its care had traceable links to slavery, there was vocal outrage from some quarters at this mere statement of fact. But like it or not, between 1640 and 1807, Britain was the dominant player in the slave trade, in which 3.1 million African people were sold into slavery and transported to the colonies in the Americas and the Caribbean to work on the plantations. Their forced labour produced the sugar, tobacco, and coffee readily consumed by the British, while the plantation owners – many of them absentees who lived a genteel life far removed from the brutal conditions on their plantations – pocketed the profits.

These profits financed all manner of finery, but a country estate was the grand prize, and between 1680 and 1730 in particular, England had a building boom, which spawned an estimated 300 estates. Some with much older heritage developed links to slavery over time, including Winston Churchill's former home Chartwell in Kent, and the Tudor Speke Hall, near Liverpool, which was purchased in 1795 by Richard Watt, who'd grown rich on the sugar and rum trade in Jamaica. Others, such as Harewood House in Yorkshire, were newly built with the direct profits of slavery. Such houses were filled with artworks and furniture that projected notions of taste and sensibility but often derived from exploitation (in the 1750s several items of mahogany furniture – a product of slave labour – were purchased for Bolsover Castle in Derbyshire), while their gardens were modelled on pastoral Arcadian fantasies that belied their origins.

Abolition and compensation

The abolition of the slave trade in 1807 did not automatically mean the emancipation of enslaved people or the end of profiting from slavery. Enslaving people was still legal, and when Britain did pass legislation outlawing slavery itself in most of its empire in 1833, the government paid out the vast sum of £20 million (40 per cent of its national yearly budget) to compensate not the enslaved, but the enslavers for the loss of their "property". The debt equated to many billions today and, shockingly, wasn't paid off by British taxpayers until 2015.

It's through these payouts that we can identify many of Britain's thousands of families who enslaved people. These connections were not always simple. At Stowe (see p.62) a bill of sale was found, dating from 1715, for 272 enslaved people and some ivory, which seems to unequivocally link Richard Temple, 1st Viscount Cobham, to slavery. But evidently family opinion on the subject became divided, as Temple had descendants who became closely involved with abolition, even while others claimed compensation.

The battle over how we interpret, represent, and come to terms with England's colonial history – from the slave trade to the British Raj in India – goes on. But if we are to fully understand the past and our cultural inheritance, we must inevitably take the bad with the good. Telling the full, unvarnished histories of England's great houses and gardens may be uncomfortable for some, but it is necessary, and long overdue.

Stowe

Built to impress, this imposing estate charts the evolution of the 18th-century English landscape garden style.

The Palladian Bridge, built in 1738 and attributed to James Gibbs, covers Charles Bridgeman's Octagon Lake

Stowe is an extraordinary expression of arrogance. This famous garden saw the rise of some of England's best-known landscape architects, including Charles Bridgeman, William Kent, and Lancelot "Capability" Brown. Although the lasting impression of their combined talent ranges from the sublime to the dull, and the experience is somewhat disjointed, Stowe is widely regarded as the most significant English landscape garden in existence.

Formal framework

Stowe's era of expansion began under Richard Temple, 1st Viscount Cobham, who employed Charles Bridgeman (from 1711) and architect John Vanbrugh (from 1719) to develop the landscape. Bridgeman's design was formal, in keeping with the style of the English Baroque park spearheaded by horticultural double act George London and Henry Wise (see p.24). He created the Octagon Lake and the Wick Quarter of formal woodland, as well as long axial vistas, or *pattes d'oie* (paths radiating out from a focal point). To these, Vanbrugh – and, later, architect James Gibbs – added eye-catchers, in the form of monuments and pavilions. Bridgeman's remarkable layout formed a framework for his successors to enhance.

Another landscaping legend, William Kent, took over around 1735, after working with Bridgeman. Kent extended Stowe into a landscape of romantic tableaux, shifting the focus from a central view to a range of vistas that could be enjoyed during a walk around the park. The suitably lustful Temple of Venus surveys the Eleven Acre Lake from one side, while on the other a rugged mock ruin, the Hermitage, draws the eye.

right The Temple of British Worthies showcases classical-style busts of the great and the good of British culture, including Shakespeare; **below** *The Oxford Bridge, comprising three arches and four urns along each parapet, spans the artificial lake Oxford Water and dates from 1761*

Palladian paradise

After falling out with "corrupt" Whig leader Robert Walpole, Cobham decided to use his garden to poke fun at his political opponents. Kent obliged, creating his theatrical masterpiece, the Elysian Fields (where, in Greek mythology, the "blessed" live after death). The Temple of Ancient Virtue peers across the river to the Temple of British Worthies, where playwright William Shakespeare rubs shoulders with scientist Isaac Newton, among other illustrious names. In the late 1730s, Kent added further fashionable elements, including the Shell Bridge and the Grotto – a novel space for entertaining.

Following Kent's death in 1748, head gardener Lancelot "Capability" Brown developed the last major part of the garden – the Grecian Valley – in the spirit of Kent's Elysian Fields. Vast new temples, including the Grecian Temple, were built, positioned to offer uninterrupted views across the park.

Gradually, Brown developed his own style. Under the patronage of Cobham's nephew, Richard Grenville-Temple, 2nd Earl Temple, he softened the landscape, giving Stowe's lakes and canals a serpentine shape and turning avenues of trees into more natural clumps. The Grecian Temple was also modified and renamed the Temple of Concord and Victory, to celebrate victory over the French in the Seven Years' War (1756–1763).

After a long decline, the house became Stowe School in 1923, and then in 1989 the National Trust took over the garden. Restoration work is ongoing, though its focus on the monuments rather than the landscape has drawn criticism. Visiting both house and garden helps to unite the two parts, however, and the mark of masters is still visible on this much-lauded landscape.

The many follies at Stowe are mostly inspired
by ancient Roman architecture, such as the
Palladian Bridge attributed to James Gibbs.
The Gothic Temple on the horizon, also designed
by Gibbs in 1741, is one of the exceptions.

Beauty and the sublime

"Sublimity is, therefore, only another word for the effect of greatness upon the feelings."

John Ruskin, Modern Painters, *1843*

Notions of beauty had filtered into the English Landscape Movement via various art forms. Classical antiquity, as seen on the Grand Tour, had offered symmetry, perfect proportions, and simple, elegant lines. Writers such as Alexander Pope and Joseph Addison had extolled the virtues of nature in their essays and epistles. And in his 1753 book *The Analysis of Beauty*, artist William Hogarth had talked of the serpentine "line of beauty" as being the source of all visual pleasure, bringing variety and movement to any composition.

The philosophy of the age had an effect too, as ideas of liberty, individualism, and intellectual freedom were winning out over formality and uniformity. The key aesthetic inspiration of the movement, however, came from a trio of 17th-century Baroque landscape painters, who provided designers with the perfect Arcadian model for their ambitious projects.

Painting the landscape

Most influential, perhaps, was French painter Claude Lorrain, whose landscapes were revered for capturing an idealized "Roman campagna", in rural fantasies populated with crumbling temples and grazing animals. Another Frenchman, Nicolas Poussin, was more in the vein of Venetian masters such as Titian, often placing mythological subjects within a classical setting. Italian painter Salvator Rosa, meanwhile, brought a darker, moodier

style to landscape painting, with jagged, towering rock faces and gnarled trees.

The profound influence these artists had on English designers has been widely acknowledged. William Kent (a painter himself) was known to be a big fan of Rosa. Henry Hoare II is thought to have laced his garden at Stourhead with direct echoes of Lorrain's paintings (see p.49). Charles Bridgeman packed as many classical follies into the garden at Stowe (see p.62) as he could. And Lancelot "Capability" Brown was the master of creating Elysian fields at Blenheim Palace and Claremont (see p.56), full of lakes, sinuous pathways, rolling lawns, woodlands, wide vistas, and Palladian monuments. All these elements could be found in the painters' compositions, and together they evoked a contrived naturalism that made deliberate reference to landscapes real and imagined.

The sublime

By the mid 18th century, the English Landscape Movement was the established style du jour, but a new aesthetic was gaining traction to rival these accepted ideals of beauty – that of the sublime. The concept was laid out by politician and philosopher Edmund Burke in a 1757 essay, which argued that beauty was something well formed and pleasing to the eye, but the sublime had the power to evoke intense feelings of wonder, awe, even terror.

Burke believed it was our sensory experiences, not rational thought, that informed our knowledge of the world, and that visions of grandeur, vastness, obscurity, and wilderness could produce in us the strongest emotions – a kind of delighted horror or astonishment. These ideas were still rooted in man's relationship with nature, and Burke would claim that

The Finding of Moses *by Salvator Rosa, c. 1660–1665, showing the dramatic landscape that would come to define the concept of the sublime in art*

The River Teme at Downton, Herefordshire, *1785-1786 by Thomas Hearne, depicts a river scene in typical Picturesque style*

Salvator Rosa, with his wilder, more rugged elements, was the "painter of the sublime". The rational beauty associated with the neoclassical English Landscape Movement was now being shaken up with notions of savagery and darkness, and it would lead to new artistic ideals that would shape the coming decades.

The Picturesque

The two concepts of beauty and the sublime came together in the style known as the Picturesque. The term was first adopted by artist and writer William Gilpin in his 1768 *Essay on Prints* to refer, somewhat literally, to "that kind of beauty which is agreeable in a picture", but he later expanded on the principles, as combining the smooth, harmonious, and ordered (the beautiful) with the rough, grandiose, and intimidating (the sublime). A Picturesque landscape would incorporate the asymmetrical, irregular, and rustic for texture and variety – a ruined castle, ideally – as well as a sense of perspective, resulting in an aesthetic experience based on instinct rather than rational thought.

With these ideas in mind, Gilpin argued that people could go in search of the Picturesque and create it themselves – find natural scenes that could be arranged and illustrated as a framed Picturesque composition. He considered Claude Lorrain's landscapes the epitome of the concept but did not believe artists had to trek across Europe to seek out such magnificent sights; Picturesque beauty could, and should, be found in England.

So, on Gilpin's advice, pleasure-seekers headed to the Lake District and along the River Wye in search of wild, majestic scenery, many of them with the latest fashionable accessory in hand: the Claude Glass. This was a darkened pocket mirror that, when held up to the landscape, framed the composition and lent it a soft tinge to help sketchers imitate the great Lorrain's style.

The Picturesque garden

The impact of the Picturesque on the English Landscape Movement was to draw it away from the symmetrical proportions and studied neoclassicism of Lancelot "Capability" Brown towards a more pictorial landscape. The wild, the natural, and the unexpected were balanced with careful composition to create a unified scene that was evocative and, quite deliberately, as pretty as a picture.

Humphry Repton was the chief proponent of this new style, advocating the creation of a foreground, middle ground, and background, whereby the focal point – around the house – could be manipulated the most, with the reintroduction of formal elements and ornamental planting. Each successive plane would then become increasingly unstructured, with parkland in the middle distance, stretching out to wilderness beyond. Though much of Repton's work entailed "improving" earlier designs by Brown and others, he did create Sheringham Park in Norfolk from scratch in 1812 using these principles, with a balustraded terrace around the house, then a serpentine park, and the blustery North Sea in the distance.

Others garden makers created their own interpretations. The scheme at scholar Richard Payne Knight's estate, Downton Castle in Herefordshire, was hailed by Repton and remains largely intact. Hawkestone Park in Shropshire, however, is more extreme. The Hill family incorporated caves, a grotto, a ruined Gothic arch, "the Awful Precipice", and a hermitage complete with real-life hermit – truly embracing the eccentricity of the Picturesque.

The new Romantics

The ideas of the Picturesque Movement would endure, feeding into the romantic sensibilities of the later 1700s and early 1800s. The darker aspects of the sublime would be picked up in the mid-1700s Gothic revival so beloved by Horace Walpole and played out at his fantasy palace Strawberry Hill in Twickenham. Meanwhile, the perfection of nature and the heightened emotions it could evoke would concern the Romantic poets William Wordsworth and Samuel Taylor Coleridge as they wandered the Lake District deep in thought and in search of the sublime. A new, quintessentially English aesthetic had been established, and it would last long into the next century.

HUMPHRY REPTON
1752–1818

After several attempts at other careers, in 1788, Humphry Repton established himself as a "Landscape Gardener" and an "Improver" of landscape parks, often tweaking existing creations by Lancelot "Capability" Brown and others. He became famous for his "Red Books" – portfolios of his designs with "before" and "after" illustrations. An adherent of the Picturesque style, his greatest success was to reintroduce formal features around estate houses, which would become an established trend during the 19th century. He also developed themed areas, such as the Chinese and American gardens at Woburn Abbey. In pioneering such changes, Repton became the link between the English Landscape Movement and the Gardenesque Movement begun by John Claudius Loudon in the early Victorian period.

Chinoiserie
and
the
East

"The Chinese excel in the art of
laying out gardens."

William Chambers, Design of Chinese Buildings,
Furniture, Dresses, Machines and Utensils, *1757*

A strong influence on more than one garden style during the 18th century was East Asia. Indeed, it may even have played a part in the development of the English Landscape Movement. In his 1685 essay *Upon the Gardens of Epicurus*, diplomat and writer Sir William Temple contrasted the then-dominant formal garden style in Europe with the natural asymmetry of Chinese gardens; he claimed that in the East there was a word for this irregularity, *sharawadgi* – a term he may either have misheard or perhaps coined, as the source has never been found, and Temple never travelled to the region himself.

Whatever the word's origins, the sharawadgi style came to mean an artful naturalism, introducing into formal gardens an organic feel by incorporating curved lines and irregular forms. Temple put these ideas into practice at his own (largely formal) garden at Moor Park in Surrey, adding a serpentine walk amid the woodland. Within a few years, a similar trick was being used at Bulstrode Park in Buckinghamshire by William Bentinck, 1st Earl of Portland, and over the coming decades, others would go further.

A taste for chinoiserie

The sharawadgi trend was compounded by the novelty and exoticism of chinoiserie that was also influencing art, architecture, and interiors throughout Europe, and this led to a taste for adding Chinese-style

View of the Wilderness &c.

buildings to English landscape gardens. The Chinese House at Stowe (see p.62) is believed to be the oldest surviving example, dating from 1738 and attributed to William Kent, who was fascinated by Temple's concept of sharawadgi. This small pavilion, with latticed windows and painted decoration, was originally raised on poles in a pond and approached via a bridge bedecked with vases of flowers, while models of Chinese ducks floated by.

These extravagant ideas soon caught on. The Chinese house at Woburn Abbey in Bedfordshire also made an appearance on an estate map in 1738. In 1747, another was added at Shugborough Hall in Staffordshire, while at Grove House, near Windsor, Richard Bateman, who was proclaimed by Horace Walpole as the English founder of the sharawadgi taste, created a beautiful pseudo-Chinese landscape of pagodas, temples, and bridges in the 1730s. By the 1750s landowners could consult specialist design books on Chinese architecture and garden ornamentation. The most popular was by architect Sir William Chambers – who had actually lived in China for two years, and who built the most famous Chinese-style building in any English garden: the Great Pagoda at Kew, in 1761. The trend for all things Eastern was now

The Great Pagoda at Kew Gardens, designed by William Chambers, painted by William Marlow in 1763

mainstream and would filter through to other garden design styles. The notions around sharawadgi were particularly taken up in the discussion around the Picturesque (see p.70), not least by Chambers himself, who in 1772 wrote his *Dissertation on Oriental Gardening*, arguing for a new kind of garden that, like the Chinese style, was full of variety and surprise to elicit an emotional response, as opposed to the "common fields" of Lancelot "Capability" Brown. Tastes were changing, but the Far East would remain a powerful influence.

Rococo

One garden trend that incorporated Chinese elements during the 18th century but did not stand the test of time was Rococo – a flamboyantly decorative and

(briefly) highly fashionable style between 1730 and 1770, which developed as a reaction to the rigid mathematical geometry of the early formal gardens. One of the downsides of the vagaries of fashion is that examples of it have largely disappeared from England, with one or two notable exceptions.

The term itself is a 20th-century construct – Rococo was not recognized as a stylistic movement at the time – but the characteristics of the aesthetic were nonetheless distinctive. Breaking away from the rigidity of Baroque formality, Rococo gardens were very much a middle-class attempt to create an impressive garden but without the lavish expense of extensive landscape gardens. On a much smaller scale, the less wealthy could still express themselves artistically with elaborate ornament, intricacy, and, as some claim, a dash of femininity. Like the interiors style that was also part of the trend (which remained in fashion far longer than the garden style), the Rococo garden was a gloriously theatrical fantasy: deliberately asymmetrical, full of contrivance, and stuffed with fanciful elements such as statuary, buildings, and playful variations on formality.

The gardens created an Arcadian world, though with statues that were contemporary, not classical, usually painted in bright colours, and often representing everyday figures such as workmen. Buildings would also be fanciful concoctions, often vivid in colour.

Chinese Pavilion in an English Garden, an 18th-century watercolour by Thomas Robins the Elder, known for his paintings of Rococo gardens, many of which no longer exist

Rococo borrowed extensively from other design styles, and played with each and every one. Chinese architecture was appropriated for its fretwork, bells, and dragons to provide exoticism; Gothic arches and alcoves were exaggerated, while rustic architecture was used in the creation of hermitages from natural materials abundant on the estate.

Rococo remnants

Rococo gardens were few and far between, and most did not last into the modern world. One of the few near-complete examples that can still be visited today is Painswick Rococo Garden near Stroud (see p.76). Much more popular were intriguing Rococo features – usually whimsical buildings – added within a broader landscape design, and several examples still exist. The Orangery at Frampton Court, Gloucestershire, is nothing short of palatial, while the Gothic summerhouse at Enville Hall in

Staffordshire has all the mystery of a haunted church. However, as with all garden movements, there was an artist who captured many of the gardens that have since been lost; in this case, Thomas Robins the Elder. Painting on velum, Robins would depict these ornate creations, and decorate the scenes with beautiful framing. His subjects included Painswick and Woodside House, which, in a coincidental twist, has more recently been owned for nearly 50 years by Elton John (who himself could be described as a modern-day Rococo figure.)

An impulse for flamboyance, playfulness, and entertainment runs deeply through all Rococo gardens; young men who could not afford a William Kent or Lancelot "Capability" Brown design could create their own pleasure gardens – their own private version of Vauxhall or Ranelagh in London – in one magical style that, even when lost, still has impact.

Frampton Court's ornamental canal and Gothic Orangery, which date back to 1750

CASE STUDY

Painswick Rococo Garden

A rare Rococo garden, Painswick exudes the flamboyance and frivolity that typifies this short-lived style.

Though it was fleeting, Rococo was a fascinating 18th-century garden design style, emerging as it did among the English middle classes as a reaction to the Italian and French-inspired formal approach. The heady concoction of Gothic, chinoiserie, and the rustic, embodied by elaborate but ethereal structures, colourful decoration, and asymmetry, is hard to find today. England's best surviving example, Painswick Rococo Garden in Gloucestershire, had all but disappeared when various paintings by artist Thomas Robins the Elder depicting the style were discovered in the 1980s. Guided by Robins' work, the 6-acre valley garden has been restored to its former glory.

Robins was commissioned by Painswick's owner, Benjamin Hyett, in 1748, having already painted several Rococo-style gardens. His Painswick piece includes curious elements not seen elsewhere, such as the pagoda, which would have been one of the earliest such Eastern-inspired creations in England (and predates architect William Chambers' work on Chinese buildings, see p.73). Positioned on a hill and rendered in startling shades of red and blue, this structure marks Painswick as a revolutionary garden. Likewise, the temple shown in Robins' work exemplifies the Strawberry Hill Gothic style yet predates it by a few years.

Fun and frolics

Radical though Hyett's new garden was, it was created purely for pleasure, filled with frivolous elements such as follies, summerhouses, and serpentine walks and laid out in an asymmetrical design intended to surprise and delight its visitors. There is no symbolism or poetry – Hyett left that to the sterner English landscape garden brigade.

left *Painting of the gardens by Thomas Robins the Elder, 1748;*
below *The Gothic summerhouse known, mysteriously, as the Eagle House*

*left The Red House – an ornate and colourful Gothic-inspired summerhouse tucked away in the woods; **centre** A view of the gardens from inside the Red House; **right** The Exedra, which melds a classical idea with Gothic architectural motifs*

Painswick is more closely allied to Buckinghamshire's Italianate bastion of pleasure, West Wycombe Park – infamous for owner Sir Francis Dashwood's secret society, the Hellfire Club. Flemish sculptor John Van Nost's statue of a naughtily characterized Pan (Greek god of the wild) at Painswick certainly hints at a connection.

Good as new

The newly reinstated garden at Painswick is a delight. At the entrance, the Eagle House folly gives commanding views across the countryside towards a Doric seat with rustic bands around its columns. Walking through the woodland planting, the Red House appears – an elaborate summerhouse with S-shaped arches and two distinct facades overlooking the garden's two straight avenue approaches. The circuit continues to the Exedra, or portico seating area, a magnificent curved, white-painted Gothic feature with views over the formal gardens, productive gardens, and pool. The new planting is ostentatious, capturing the essence of the colourful borders painted by Robins, which are so detailed they have led some to speculate that the artist himself had a hand in the garden's design.

Rococo has long been derided as a style; writing in *The World* periodical in 1753, satirist Francis Coventry brutally dismissed it as representative of his character Squire Mushroom's middle-class aspirations to grandeur. But Painswick Rococo Garden is not pretentious – it is delightful, fanciful, and utterly capricious. The style is better viewed as a reaction to the political dominance of France in the run-up to the Seven Years' War (1756–1763). Rococo gardens were not built to last, though, and were it not for the record Robins created, they would have been entirely lost to nature.

Pleasure gardens

"Chaises, grotto, fishing, all in perfection."

Earl Temple of Stowe, c.1766, The National Archives

Throughout the 20th century and beyond, the landscapes typical of Lancelot "Capability" Brown lent themselves perfectly to the vogue for country house hotels and golf courses, but in the 18th century, when many of these gardens were first created, what did the landed gentry and their upper-class visitors actually *do* with the gardens they had spent so much money on?

The most common usage was simply to admire and enjoy the vast spaces – on foot, on horseback, or in a carriage – and for the leisured classes, the carriage was obviously the least tiring option, particularly popular with the ladies dressed in their finery, but health and exercise were a consideration too.

In the Georgian era, doctors recommended swimming in naturally cold water. Dr George Cheyne, regarded as Britain's leading expert on the treatment of "hypochondria" among the landed gentry, prescribed regular immersion in cold plunge pools in the 1720s, and estate owners gladly obliged. Setting the fashion, banker Henry Hoare II would describe a summer's day "souse" in his cold pool in his newly built grotto at Stourhead, Wiltshire, as "Asiatick luxury". Elsewhere, in gardens such as Rousham (see p.52), Prior Park, and Painswick (see p.76), swimmers would bathe naked in the open air, frolicking gaily (normally screened by evergreen shrubs) in stone-edged circular pools that are still visible today.

Aristocratic angling

Other rustic pursuits available to the wealthy estate master were perhaps more calming. Eighteenth-century paintings show the nouveau riche angling *en famille* in their well-stocked lakes and ponds, or simply posing, rod in hand, in group images known as conversation pieces. By this time, however, angling was an activity that required comfort, and so the fishing lodge, built over the water, developed. Some of the oldest surviving examples date from the Elizabethan period, but the

Georgians perfected the design, the finest surely being the Fishing Pavilion at Kedleston Hall, in Derbyshire, created by Robert Adam in 1770–1772. You enter into a smart dining room where fish-themed paintings adorn the walls, while the large sash windows offer the splendid option of fishing without leaving the building! With a boathouse and cold bath beneath, this really was a relaxing day away from the hall for landowners and a few select guests to enjoy.

Outdoor delights

The gardens were used for plenty more pleasurable activities besides: sailing, reading, playing with telescopes, practising archery, music, dressing up – and escaping the prying eyes of the household staff to enjoy amorous assignations. The clues were there in the often-missed erotic references in several gardens, chief among them the ribald pleasure palace of West Wycombe, home to Sir Francis Dashwood and his notorious Hellfire Club.

Dashwood created one of the most explicit of all garden features, now lost, by laying out a central mound with two hillocks, each topped with red planting and a triangular shrubby entrance, designed to evoke a recumbent naked woman – an apt setting for the Hellfire Club's debauched parties. The X-rated theme continued in the Temple of Venus, which stood upon a belly-like mound with an anatomically shaped entrance to the

above Engraving of West Wycombe Park by William Woollett, c. 1750s; **left** The racy Temple of Venus at West Wycombe Park, rebuilt to Sir Francis Dashwood's original suggestive design in the 1980s

carved-out chamber beneath and a statue of the Roman god Mercury above – a conscious play on the noxious treatment for syphilis to warn visitors of the possible consequences of their pleasure.

Such carefully manicured gardens did not just provide beautiful vistas; they were playgrounds for the wealthy, where all whims, eccentricities, and obsessions could be, and were, indulged.

plants and

planting:

the golden

"The duty we owe to our gardens is to so use the plants that they shall form beautiful pictures; and that, while delighting our eyes."

Gertrude Jekyll, Colour in the Flower Garden, *1908*

afternoon

Parks and arboreta

"Breathing places for the metropolis."

John Claudius Loudon, Gardener's Magazine, *1829*

Before the 1840s there were no public parks in Britain's towns. Estate parklands and pleasure gardens were accessible only to those who could afford the fee, and before the Industrial Revolution most towns were close enough to the fields beyond for such spaces to feel unnecessary. Dedicated parks that were publicly owned and free to access had not yet been created. So as sprawling development encroached upon the surrounding countryside, urban inhabitants found themselves increasingly separated from the natural world.

The shift occurred in the 1830s. In this rigidly class-based Victorian society, as town populations boomed with the influx of labourers in search of more work and better wages, the upper-class reformers and town planners became interested in the notion of "rational recreation" as a method of social reform. A report by the Select Committee on Public Walks of 1833 made clear the thinking: that by bringing an element of the countryside into urban spaces, with areas for walking, exercising, and relaxing, they could bolster the health and happiness of the "middle and humbler classes", bringing moral improvement and aesthetic value to the area in the process.

Derby Arboretum

By the late 1830s London's royal parks had begun to open to the public, but it was the Derby Arboretum, opened in 1840, that would be dubbed "Britain's first public park". The arboretum was built on land donated by Joseph Strutt, a renowned industrialist and the former mayor of Derby, primarily as a "thank you" to the townspeople for enabling his family to amass its vast wealth.

Strutt commissioned John Claudius Loudon – botanist, landscape architect, and prolific author – to design the park.

Loudon was a true Renaissance Man in garden history terms. He was the first to record the term "arboretum" as a collection of plants, particularly trees, for botanical research, and as a city planner he was a passionate believer in the need for green spaces to act as lungs as well as recreational spaces in urban environments.

Strutt's original plan was for a botanical garden, but the pair compromised and the final result was a botanical garden set amid public pleasure grounds. Throughout the 11-acre site, Loudon put into practice his design theory of the "Gardenesque", not imitating nature as the English Landscape Movement had, but incorporating artificial elements, such as exotic plants, gravel walkways, seating, geometric flowerbeds, fountains, statues, and pavilions. Above all, of course, there was greenery, including 1,000 trees and 100 types of rose, all carefully labelled.

In his inaugural speech on opening day, Strutt emphasized his motivation for creating the arboretum: to provide an area for recreation and exercise in the fresh air and to educate visitors through the collection of valuable trees and shrubs on display. It was a noble vision, though not yet a fully egalitarian one. Initially, an entrance fee was charged to pay for the maintenance of the park; however, as this was obviously prohibitive for the less well-off, entry would be free on Sundays and Wednesdays, when workers had their days off. The charge was eventually abolished entirely in 1882.

The Victorian parks movement

The Derby Arboretum, if not wholly a public park to begin with, would nonetheless prove a great inspiration to other towns wanting to create parks that truly were for everyone. Numerous examples sprang up in the ensuing decades, particularly in the larger industrial cities of the North, including Liverpool's Prince's Park in 1842 and Birkenhead Park in 1847 (both designed by Joseph Paxton of Chatsworth fame), and the People's Park, Halifax, in 1857. The Victorian parks movement would offer city dwellers tranquil lakes, lush woodlands, decorative flowerbeds, and ornamental features that they could not easily access otherwise.

Indeed, such was the attraction of this new urban feature that its influence would spread internationally. Derby Arboretum was one of several parks Frederick Law Olmsted visited in 1859, while on a tour around Europe in preparation for his plans for New York's Central Park. It is widely acknowledged that he incorporated many of its elements into his final design.

Public parks are now firmly recognized as essential components of urban life, increasingly cherished as our awareness of the threats of pollution and climate change grows. Many Victorian parks were allowed to decline during the 20th century, but efforts are now being made to restore and protect these spaces. Derby Arboretum is a case in point. In 2002, a fine restoration project began, and it is now credited as one of the finest tree collections in England.

The
rise
of the
nursery

"They spare no expense in collecting the choicest sort and greatest variety ... from every quarter of the globe."

John Middleton on Chelsea nurserymen, View of the Agriculture of Middlesex, *1798*

Between the mid 1700s and the early 1900s, a remarkable 25 nurseries had their premises on the King's Road. Chelsea had been an established market-gardening area since the early 17th century, supplying London's constant desire for fresh produce, but the westward spread of suburban development, particularly during the 19th century, made such extensive land use too expensive to maintain. So, as a new fashion for exotic plants emerged and landowners realized they could charge higher rents from nurseries, which needed less retail space due to growing their stock outside the city, the nursery trade flourished, with the King's Road as its epicentre.

The exotic nursery

The exact origin of the trend is hard to pinpoint, but perhaps the first trace dates back to the 1780s, when the extraordinary Countess of Strathmore, Mary Eleanor Bowes – a trained botanist – was building glasshouses and hothouses on her estate at the magnificent Stanley Grove on the King's Road, to house her fashionable collection of exotic plants. Following a scandal-ridden divorce case and then the Countess's death in 1800, Stanley Grove was sold, and in 1808 a portion of the grounds was purchased by Joseph Knight, who used it as the basis for his new nursery.

Joseph Knight's Exotic Nursery rapidly became successful, supported as it was by the leading horticulturalist of the day, John Claudius Loudon. In his *Gardener's Magazine* he described the richness and superiority of Knight's plants and excessively praised the heated conservatory at the centre of the nursery, which happened to have been designed by Loudon himself. Knight would sponsor plant-hunting expeditions across the world, and so the plants he displayed included orange trees, camellias, and rhododendrons, as well as a vast collection of exotics such as proteas, fuchsias, and pineapples. His King's Road nursery was at the very centre of horticultural innovation and established the area as the foremost destination for fashionable garden retail.

After Knight's death in 1855 his nursery was sold to the master nurseryman of England, James Veitch, who changed its name to the Royal Exotic Nursery and established it as the base for his family business. Aided by its proximity to the Chelsea Physic Gardens, the Veitch nursery was hugely successful and continued until 1914.

The new nurserymen

Although the name Veitch's would come to dominate as an internationally renowned brand, many of the nurseries established along the King's Road from the late 1700s onwards were household names in England. Nurseries such as Colvill's and Davey's, famed for their majestic flowers, and later Bull's, known for "new and rare" plants, especially

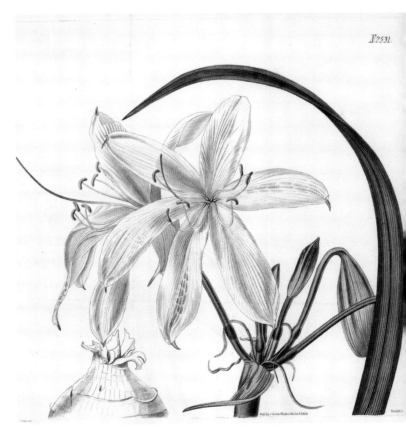

orchids, and Wimsett's, supplied the affluent Chelsea owners of suburban villas and luxury country estates with the unusual flowers, trees, and shrubs that had become so popular.

Eventually, however, most of these establishments would be absorbed by the burgeoning growth of west London. By the advent of the 20th century, only Veitch's, Wimsett's, and Bull's remained, but even they did not survive the outbreak of the First World War – one by one they closed, the last vast nurseries in London, ending the line begun by the Brompton Park Nursery in Kensington (see p.24) and the Loddiges Nursery in Hackney.

Botanical illustration of the Australian lily, Crinum arenarium, *drawn at Joseph Knight's Exotic Nursery on the King's Road, 1824*

The Loddiges of Hackney

Hackney didn't first become fashionable when it was discovered by Millennials. Several centuries ago, when it was more a village on the outskirts of the City, it was at the very heart of horticultural fashion as home to one of the most famous and successful nurseries of the 18th and 19th centuries, owned by the Loddiges family. A highly influential gardening dynasty, the Loddiges were at the very pinnacle of plant introductions, as well as technological innovation. Founded in the mid 1700s by German émigré Joachim Conrad Loddiges, the nursery first made a name for itself as a seed company supplying the major botanical gardens and estates of Europe. By the 1760s Loddiges was working with

renowned plant hunters like John and William Bartram, who were at the forefront of collecting in North America, to introduce scores of exotic new plants to the UK, including rhubarb, the original kalmia, the common rhododendron, and magnolias.

It was Conrad's son, George Loddiges, who would push the nursery to even greater heights. By the early 19th century, its site in Hackney covered 15 acres, including a 9-acre arboretum, and attracted many illustrious supporters. Charles Darwin is known to have visited, John Claudius Loudon was a vocal advocate, and the imperial gardens of St Petersburg in Russia were on the client list. Such was the nursery's success that it produced 20 issues of its own illustrated catalogue,

" The progress of this stupendous plant through the metropolis, and the effect of the broad foliage – sometimes sweeping the three-storey windows of the houses – will not easily be forgotten. "

Illustrated London News, *5 August 1854*

The Botanical Cabinet, which displayed fabulous coloured plates, many by George himself, of the thousands of new plants Conrad Loddiges & Sons had introduced.

Technological innovators

It was in the 1820s that George Loddiges would design the nursery's greatest attraction: the world's largest hothouse. This steam-heated palm house with its overhead irrigation system had the feel of a jungle, standing 12 m (40 ft) high and housing the nursery's impressive tropical plant collection – including 280 species of palm and 1,916 orchids. A magnificent sight according to visitors, the structure dwarfed all its rivals and predated the Palm House at Kew by decades – indeed, Kew would borrow the technology when it came to build its own in 1848.

The Loddiges were also involved in the single-most important advance in the transportation of live plants: the wardian case. Named after physician and naturalist Nathaniel Ward, who discovered in 1829 that plants survived and indeed thrived in a protected microclimate under glass, the wardian case was lauded as a game changer.

As Ward's plant supplier, George Loddiges was quick to test out his client's innovation, demonstrating in 1833 that in these glass cases his plants could survive the months-long journey from London to Sydney – and so a fundamental shift in global ecology began.

Like many others, the Loddiges' nursery was swept away by urban redevelopment in 1852–1854, with many of its rare and valuable plants sold off at auction – a sad end to a horticultural tour de force. When the nursery closed, the Loddiges famously transported a giant palm tree (a rare Mauritius Fan specimen, thought to have previously belonged to Empress Josephine of France) across London, to the newly opened Crystal Palace glasshouse. A team of twenty horses were needed to drag the huge palm in its special transportation box across the city.

The Loddiges dynasty, though largely unheard of today, had a seismic effect on both gardening and British culture, introducing plants from across the Empire to the sitting rooms of Victorian homes – plants, it should be remembered, that we are still enjoying today.

Plant hunters and collectors

"You will begin to think shortly I manufacture
pines at my pleasure..."

David Douglas, Letter to William Hooker, 1831

Many of the plants that feature in English gardens today are not native species – they have travelled across the globe, transported by the "plant hunters" of the 19th and early 20th centuries. These explorers of the plant world would go on adventures in search of the most exotic, floriferous species, and the plants they brought back would transform our gardens. Their findings made British nurseries and botanical gardens ever-more competitive, eager to be the first to obtain the latest discoveries.

The botanical explorers

A key forerunner was the intrepid David Douglas, a Scottish botanist who made three expeditions to North America for the Horticultural Society of London (later the Royal Horticultural Society) and introduced over 200 species to England, the most famous of which, the Douglas fir, bears his name. However, such expeditions weren't easy: having survived a bear attack, snow-blindness, and several near-drownings, he met a grizzly end in Hawaii in 1834, aged just 35, at the bottom of a pit trap.

Robert Fortune was hired as Douglas's replacement by the Horticultural Society, which, in 1843, after much deliberation, dispatched him to China armed with two pistols. Fortune would gather an incredible collection of clematis, viburnums, and honeysuckles, though he too returned with alarming tales of piracy and near-death experiences.

Another collector, Ernest Wilson, was commissioned by Harry Veitch, of the successful King's Road nursery dynasty, to bring back a living specimen of the white-flowered handkerchief tree from China in 1899. After many disappointments, and under dreadful conditions, Wilson managed the task, returning in 1902 with numerous other prized specimens such as jasmines, forsythias, and mahonias. Indeed, during his 30-year career, Wilson brought over 2,000 species to the UK, 60 of which bear his name. His introductions would inspire the creation of many collectors' gardens.

The Garden Society

One of the greatest collectors of the period was George Forrest, a Scottish botanist who in the early 20th century collected tens of thousands of specimens from China, including many rhododendrons, and uncovered more than 1,000 species that were new to science. Forrest was sponsored mostly by the Garden Society, a secretive group of the most influential garden makers, botanists, and collectors of the day.

The Garden Society's significance as one of the main sponsors of the plant hunters, alongside Kew and the Royal Botanic Garden Edinburgh, cannot be underplayed. Members included Arthur Bulley, creator of the Ness Botanic Gardens in Cheshire, and the Messel family, who developed the gardens at Nymans (see p.92). They were a competitive bunch, and it is them we can thank for the introduction

Plant hunter George Forrest and Lao Chao (Zhao Chengzhang), head of his collecting team, in China, c.1925

of major plants such as rhododendrons, azaleas, and camellias, among others.

Without the activities of plant hunters and their voracious sponsors, our gardens today would look very different. However, it should be acknowledged that, as with many activities associated with British imperialism, the practice of plant hunting had little regard for the original environment from which the plants or seeds were taken. The primary concern was the customer – the Victorian plant collectors, whose obsessions with acquiring new plant species trumped all else.

Obsession and collections

As plant hunters scoured the world for new and exciting plant specimens, the 19th and early 20th centuries saw a massive rise in plant collecting. The influx of new plants into Britain, be they ferns, camellias, rhododendrons, or lilies, sparked the imagination and triggered obsessions among botanists both amateur and professional, and those with the means began to develop extensive private collections.

Autumn colour at the Westonbirt Arboretum in Gloucestershire, which is home to five national tree collections

National collecting

With their love of science, cataloguing, and ostentation, Victorian collectors became increasingly competitive when it came to beating their rivals to the latest botanical status symbol: the most exotic or attractive version of a plant for their garden, greenhouse, or indeed home. With intrepid plant hunters answering the call and venturing across the world to bring back literally thousands of new species, many gardens were created based upon the obsessive interests of the owner.

Indeed, in some cases entire gardens were made solely to grow a range of species and all its variants. Sheringham Park in Norfolk, for example, began collecting rhododendrons as early as 1850 and now holds one of the national collections, with over 80 species of rhododendron and azalea. The collection was extended by Thomas Upchner, Sheringham Park's final owner before it was acquired by the National Trust, who

would sponsor the plant collector Ernest Wilson in his search for Chinese species. Wilson's introductions would inspire the creation of many collectors' gardens, including the Isabella Plantation in London's Richmond Park, which holds the national collection of evergreen "Wilson 50" Kurume azaleas – so named after the 50 species introduced from Japan by Wilson in the 1920s.

Many fine arboreta were also established in England during the Victorian period, often due to the expeditions of plant hunter David Douglas, most of which are still in existence today. The arboreta obsession gripped many wealthy 19th-century landowners; in particular Robert Holford, who would establish Westonbirt Arboretum in Gloucestershire from 1829 onwards, with collections of rhododendrons, azaleas, camellias, and magnolias, as well as impressive trees such as the giant Wellingtonia and Western red cedar introduced from America, all planted in the Picturesque style (see p.70). Later, from 1886, Algernon Freeman-Mitford, Lord Redesdale (grandfather of the Mitford sisters), would bring his passion for East Asia to the Cotswolds in the magnificently naturalistic Batsford Arboretum, with significant collections of Japanese maples, pines, magnolias, and bamboos.

Nymans

Public display, whether in arboretums, parks, or botanic gardens, was an important element in collecting – a way to show off

> " There is a mysterious delight in the discovery of a new species, akin to that of seeing for the first time... plants or animals of which one has till then only read. "

Charles Kingsley, Glaucus; or, The Wonders of the Shore, *1890*

wealth, status, and scientific knowledge. But a private garden might also become home to these exciting new plant discoveries. One of the great Edwardian examples, which is known primarily as an outstanding showcase for its incredible plant collections, is Nymans in West Sussex.

The house has a truly romantic feel as it is partially a ruin, destroyed by fire in 1947, while the gardens, developed from the late 19th century by three generations of the Messel family, contain vast collections from three key plant hunters of the 20th century, George Forrest, Frank Kingdon-Ward, and Harold Comber, who was the son of Nymans' head gardener, James Comber. Nymans has many plants associated with Harold Comber's plant-hunting trips. Uniquely for the time, he focused on South America and Tasmania, bringing back specimens well suited to the sheltered microclimate at Nymans. Their collection of Chilean plants is second only to the Royal Botanic Garden Edinburgh in the UK.

Fern mania

The ability to easily display a collection would also be a significant factor in encouraging the obsession that Victorians are perhaps most associated with: ferns. The term *pteridomania*, or "fern madness", was coined by priest, novelist, historian – and Charles Darwin's friend – Charles Kingsley in 1855 to describe the new craze that was sweeping the country at the time. Thanks largely to the development of the wardian case (see p.89), these fascinating foliage plants could be grown and displayed with ease and elegance, and with that came a fashion among serious botanists and hobbyists alike that would be expressed indoors as much as outdoors.

The fern motif would be used in fabrics, wallpapers, furniture carving, and much more, while the plant itself – enclosed in its trusty wardian case, safe from the pollution of the 19th-century air (a method that would enable another Victorian collecting craze: orchids) – would be proudly exhibited in elegant drawing rooms across England, Europe, and America. Though often referred to as an "English eccentricity", *pteridomania* had, like many other plant obsessions, travelled far beyond England and would long outlive our green-fingered Victorian forebears.

Azaleas and ferns along a streamlet in Isabella Plantation in London's Richmond Park, a Victorian woodland garden known for its impressive collection of evergreen azaleas.

Japan

"The whole country here is covered with nursery-gardens."

Robert Fortune, Yedo and Peking, *1863*

From 1633 to 1853, Japan closed itself off from the rest of the world. When it reopened its borders in 1854, the English rushed to explore the culture that had been hidden for two centuries. One of the first plant collectors allowed to enter Japan was John Gould Veitch of the famed Veitch nursery (see p.87). In 1860, having based himself in Nagasaki, he collected a vast array of new plants – so many, in fact, that Kew lists them in their hundreds: 232 orchids, 500 greenhouse plants, 118 exotic ferns, over 50 conifers, 153 deciduous trees, 72 evergreen and climbing shrubs, and 122 herbaceous plants. Among them were Japanese larch and dwarf maples, *Magnolia stellata* – and *Lilium auratum*, the display of which at Veitch's nursery would draw queues of several thousands.

Such was the frenzy sparked by Veitch's collection that while in Japan he fell into fierce competition with fellow plant hunter Robert Fortune, who was working for a rival nursery. Both were sending plants, seeds, and cones back to England in an effort to outdo each other, though because they shared a ship to carry their spoils home there was some confusion as to their individual achievements. Both claimed, for example, to have discovered the dwarf conifer *Chamaecyparis pisifera*.

A new influence

Amid this influx of new plants, and the trend for all things "Japonisme", it was architect Josiah Conder who introduced Japanese gardens to England, after working as a professor in the country. His 1893 book *Landscape Gardening in Japan* became the go-to reference for avid gardeners rushing to re-create their own slice of Japan. A meditative feel was key, with water, islands, bridges, and natural stone as core elements, and characteristic planting of azaleas, hostas, rhododendrons, maples, and cherries.

Recognizing its newfound allure, Japan sought to boost its global appeal and develop trade with Europe by sponsoring the Japan–British Exhibition of 1910, at London's White City – an event that attracted over 8 million visitors during its near five-month run. The most popular attractions were the two Japanese display gardens, the Garden of Peace and the

Garden of Floating Islands, which covered 11 acres with extensive lakes and cascades. Such was the desire for complete authenticity that all elements, even the rocks, were imported from Japan, while vast painted canvas scenes were positioned behind the gardens to reflect the Japanese obsession with the "borrowed" landscape. The "Pigmy Trees" exhibit also proved a fascination to visitors, showcasing over 2,000 bonsai specimens that ranged from 20 to over 300 years old.

The gardens were a major success. Their aim, to emphasize the shared love of horticulture between Japan and Britain, was widely reported, and trace elements even survive to this day. The stone bridge from the Garden of Peace is still visible in Hammersmith Park, while the scaled-down replica of the beautifully carved Gateway of the Imperial Messenger of Kyoto's Nishi Hongan-ji Temple, the Chokushi-Mon, was rehoused in Kew Gardens. It's thought the show was also a direct influence on Alan de Tatton, who created a Japanese tea garden with a Western twist at Tatton Park soon after his visit. Restored in 2001, it is still considered one of the finest Japanese gardens in Europe.

The Japanese garden in England

The English fascination with Japanese gardens has remained a constant since the 19th century, and although some modern examples tend towards the formulaic, there are many across the country where authenticity is still rigorously adhered to.

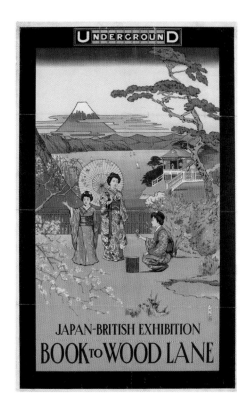

A poster by John Henry Lloyd advertising the Japan-British Exhibition held in London's White City in 1910

The Japanese Garden at St Mawgan, Cornwall, winds through a lush wooded valley that looks particularly magnificent in autumn when the 100-plus varieties of maple change colour. It also boasts traditional features such as a tea house, koi pond, moss garden, and fine *karensansui* – Zen dry stone garden. The glorious tea garden at the Newt in Somerset, meanwhile, harks back to the 17th-century Chishakuin temple garden in Kyoto, with a bamboo entrance gate, water features, and a stunning display of mature bonsai trees.

And, of course, no Chelsea Flower Show today would be complete without the master of Japanese garden design, Kazuyuki Ishihara; his multiple gold medals over the years reflect an enduring enthusiam for Japanese gardens as tranquil spaces to retreat to in troubling times.

Italy returns

"In the midst of the most romantic grounds ... the most perfect Italian palace you can conceive."

Benjamin Disraeli, writing on Deepdene House, the Disraeli Letters, iii. 1104, *1840*

While Humphry Repton had reintroduced terraces and ornamentation such as urns and balustrades into the landscape garden designs of the late 18th and early 19th centuries, he can hardly be said to have created Italianate gardens. His disciple, however, the Scottish botanist, landscape architect, and author John Claudius Loudon, certainly did.

Loudon's influence

In 1819, Loudon set off on a tour of Europe, primarily France and Italy, to gather information for his planned magnum opus, *An Encyclopaedia of Gardening*. Loudon particularly admired the geometric terraces characteristic of so many Italian gardens, sketching them and writing notes on them throughout his trip. He was particularly entranced by the famous Botanical Garden at Padua in northern Italy – the world's oldest, dating from 1545.

Loudon's travels in Italy helped him formulate his theory of the "Gardenesque" style, which was an attempt to bring order back into English gardens after a century of naturalism with the English Landscape Movement. He believed gardens should be works of art, easily distinguishable from the naturalistic growth favoured by the Picturesque style (see p.70) – ideas he wrote about in his successful periodical, the *Gardener's Magazine*. Gardens, he argued, should be places for cultivation, where the hand of man was evident, advocating the planting of non-native species in circular flowerbeds and distancing himself from the serpentine line of the landscape garden.

The Gardenesque in practice

Loudon's *Encyclopaedia* was published in 1822 and his ideas were quick to catch on. In 1825 architect William Atkinson created what is regarded as the first Italian-style garden of the 19th

A view of the Italianate gardens at Deepdene House in Surrey, photographed in 1870. The house and the gardens are now lost

century at Deepdene House, Surrey, with terraces, balustrades, steps, and sculpture. Loudon was impressed, and a new trend duly began for adding Italianate terraces to landscape gardens, led by architect Charles Barry, who did just that at Trentham Gardens in Staffordshire in 1834, and many other estates besides.

It was not until after Loudon's death in 1843 that the term "Gardenesque" was developed further, with the leading lights of Victorian garden design, Joseph Paxton, Edward Milner, and Edward Kemp, melding the English Landscape and Italianate styles in their designs. Paxton especially was a keen follower of Loudon's ideas, demonstrating at Chatsworth how Italianate straight lines should be used around the house to harmonize with the architecture, with softer planting borrowed from the Picturesque style beyond.

This mix of styles established the formula for parks throughout England – such as Birkenhead, designed by Paxton and supervised by Kemp – as well as private gardens. Paxton, Milner, and Kemp would inspire many designers of the early

20th century, with the Italian influence re-emerging in the Arts and Crafts Movement, notably in the work of Thomas Mawson and Harold Peto. Elegant structural elements now blended with romantic cottage planting to create a style that, though Italian at heart, was quintessentially English in spirit.

HAROLD PETO
1854–1933

After a long career as an architect, Harold Peto turned his immaculate eye to garden design after meeting gardener William Robinson. Peto would go on to combine the best of Arts and Crafts gardens with his love of the Italian Renaissance, creating beautifully terraced gardens softened with natural planting and punctuated by cypresses, urns, sarcophagi, and statuary. The garden at his home, Iford Manor, was one of the masterpieces of 20th-century design and acted as a kind of "shop window" that perfectly expressed his style.

Iford Manor gardens, with Italianate statuary and yews punctuating the herbaceous borders. The gardens were created by Harold Peto, who lived at Iford from 1899 to 1933.

The Arts and Crafts garden

"Our gardens are beautiful in proportion
to their truth to nature."

William Robinson, The Garden, *1872*

In reaction to the rapid industrialization of England throughout the Victorian and Edwardian eras, the Arts and Crafts Movement – which dominated from the late 19th to the early 20th century – championed a return to honest simplicity in design, handcraftsmanship, and the pre-industrial principles of the past, particularly the medieval, Elizabethan, and Jacobean periods.

Although principally known for its architecture, furniture, fabrics, art, and utilitarian products – encapsulated most famously in the work of William Morris – the movement also brought about a fundamental change in how we designed, planted, and viewed our gardens. This new style, with its portrayal of a romanticized rural England and its marriage of use and beauty, would return us to the forefront of contemporary garden making and have a worldwide influence that would dominate right up to the present day.

Formality versus romanticism

One of the Arts and Crafts Movement's greatest advocates, who still influences the modern planting style of designers such as Tom Stuart-Smith, Andy Sturgeon, and Dan Pearson, was William Robinson (see p.104). It was he who argued against the Victorian formality of carpet bedding and the heavy maintenance and propagation of the newly introduced half-hardy annuals in bold colours, sparking a fierce debate known as "the battle of the styles" with

above *Verbenas, persicarias, and dahlias in the perennial borders at William Robinson's former home Gravetye Manor in Sussex;* **right** *Heleniums, cannas, and stipa offer contrasting textures in the borders at Gravetye for the naturalistic effect advocated in Arts and Crafts gardens*

architectural formalists such as Reginald Blomfield. Robinson argued instead for the mixed herbaceous border with natural-looking drifts of perennials, shrubs, and grasses that would evoke an idyllic view of England on a golden summer's afternoon. The resolution of these two aesthetics would be found in the Arts and Crafts

---

WILLIAM ROBINSON

1838–1935

Belligerent and opinionated, plantsman and prolific author William Robinson railed against the Italianate formality of the high-Victorian period, championing instead the naturalistic planting of native herbaceous perennials in abundant drifts in the English cottage garden and Arts and Crafts style. He is hailed as the forebear of contemporary planting. Robinson implemented his naturalistic planting ideas at his Elizabethan home, Gravetye Manor, in Sussex. In the woodland, Robinson planted swathes of daffodils and cyclamen, while establishing Japanese anemones, lilies, acanthus, and pampas grass in the cleared surrounding areas. He built an oval walled productive garden that still impresses today, plus individual heather gardens and water gardens for his beloved waterlilies. Gravetye is now a fine hotel, but the gardens still excel, maintaining the layout and planting principles laid down by Robinson.

garden, and it was Gertrude Jekyll (see p.106), in collaboration with architect Edwin Lutyens, and Thomas Mawson, who would exemplify the new vision.

In combining the naivety and charm of cottage gardens in their wild abundance with the evocative romanticism and architectural formality of the country house garden, the Arts and Crafts style engaged strong notions of English national identity, despite the overriding influence coming from Italy (see p.98). The strong demarcation throughout – created by yew hedges, topiary, Elizabethan formality in beds and borders, and swathes of climbing roses billowing around walls, gazebos, and gateways – as well as the stated desire to use local materials and crafts, appealed to a nation that was witnessing the loss of its empire and economic status.

The masterpiece of the style is Rodmarton Manor in the Cotswolds, designed by architect Ernest Barnsley for the Biddulph family. Working with Margaret Biddulph and her head gardener, Barnsley created both house and gardens strictly adhering to the Arts and Crafts principles, with garden rooms featuring topiary, fruit and vegetables, romantic garden pavilions, and the finest herbaceous borders. It was a lengthy build, hand-worked by local craftsmen, lasting from 1909 until 1929, three years after Barnsley's death, but Rodmarton remains his great legacy; the gardens – which are still largely unchanged – are an essential pilgrimage for all students of the style.

Restorative power

It was a nostalgia for England and what was seen as its glorious past as a great nation, as well as the shocking post-traumatic stress suffered by so many military men during the First World War, that led to the golden era of Arts and Crafts gardens in the early 1900s. Some of the most notable gardens were newly established when these men went off to war in 1914, and they provided a safe haven for many of the wealthy country estate owners who were lucky enough to return. Many of England's most popular, indeed iconic, gardens were developed during this period by military men who sought the solace of nature, the time to recuperate, and the sanctuary of cultivating the new plant introductions from China and South America. They include Hidcote Manor in the Cotswolds by Major Lawrence Johnston, Borde Hill Gardens in West Sussex by Colonel Stephenson R. Clarke, and the remarkable Cothay Manor in Somerset, created by Lieutenant-Colonel Reginald Cooper, which remains hardly altered. It was certainly not a privilege available to every soldier; the working-class chap who returned to suburbia or the urban squalor of the city had no such welcome home.

Yet it is these notions of Englishness, the apparent stability that "old" gardens can offer by harking back to the past, and the evocation of comfort and home in the cottage garden elements that together constitute the overwhelming appeal of Arts and Crafts gardens. They are an idealized model that everyone, be they estate owner or suburban homeowner, can understand and emulate. This is surely why the style still resonates, appealing to so many gardeners and designers today, and ensuring the survival of the great originals.

Topiary and lime trees in the formal Winter Garden at Rodmarton Manor in the Cotswolds, designed by architect Ernest Barnsley

Munstead Wood

Of the more than 400 gardens Gertrude Jekyll designed, her own garden at Munstead Wood is the brightest example of her painterly application of colour.

Home to garden maker, artist, and writer Gertrude Jekyll for more than 30 years, Munstead Wood, near Godalming in Surrey, is the iconic Jekyll garden. It was also the first in a series of influential collaborations with Arts and Crafts architect Edwin Lutyens.

Jekyll bought the plot of land across the road from her mother's house in 1882 and began to create a garden, reporting her progress in articles for fellow horticultural genius William Robinson's journal *The Garden* and, later, for *Country Life*. Robinson shared many of Jekyll's design aspirations, including her more natural approach to planting. Munstead Wood soon became synonymous with Jekyll's garden style, which remains popular today.

Dream team

Jekyll was an active supporter of Surrey's suffrage movement (see p.114), alongside her friend Maria Theresa Villiers, better known as garden writer Mrs C.W. Earle, and Earle's niece, Emily (née Bulwer-Lytton), who was married to Lutyens. Munstead Wood was one of Lutyens' first commissions. Built of local stone in the "Surrey style", with dormer windows and tall chimneys, the house's architectural formality was the perfect counterpart to Jekyll's cottage garden planting, which was inspired by her travels around the area.

The garden was Jekyll's laboratory: here, she would trial her planting style and different combinations of textures and colours. An admirer of J.M.W. Turner (known as the "painter of light" for his theoretical colour wheels) and a lifelong painter herself, Jekyll applied her knowledge of colour to planting. Indeed, she preferred to be described as an "artist-gardener" rather than a "garden designer".

above *The main border at Munstead Wood;* **right** *The south border by watercolourist Helen Allingham RWS, c. 1900. Allingham met Jekyll in the 1880s; the two became friends and Jekyll invited Allingham to paint her garden at its height. This is one of nine in the series*

above *The Three Corner Garden at Munstead Wood;* **right** *The north court, pictured in May 2022;* **far right** *Jekyll's plan for the Spring Garden, from her book* Colour Schemes for the Flower Garden, *first published in 1908*

Artistic touch

The house sits at the centre of the garden plot, encircled by formal lawns, which have been neatly mown in the striped pattern that is now so evocative of an English garden. Jekyll applied her painterly colour theory to the surrounding herbaceous borders, where she used yellow and blue flowers to create a sense of light, and contrasted cool blue flowers and grey foliage with bold reds and oranges for impact. The formal design of these "rooms" recedes into a more naturalistic style of planting as you meander into the surrounding woodland.

Jekyll created several seasonal gardens, including "June" and "Spring", stressing the importance of year-round colour. She turned the lower field into a kitchen garden and developed a plant nursery, from which she supplied plants to clients and visitors. She also bred improved varieties of the plants she used most, such as *Pulmonaria angustifolia* 'Munstead Blue'.

Country Life magazine visited Munstead Wood in 1921 and this, along with the coverage given to the garden by Henry Avray Tipping in his 1925 book *English Gardens*, propelled Jekyll to fame. In her own articles, she offered advice and inspiration to the burgeoning middle-class gardener.

Jekyll received the Victoria Medal of Honour and the Veitch Memorial Medal from the Royal Horticultural Society, cementing her position as one of the most significant women in horticulture. She stood at the epicentre of a postwar England trying to establish itself in a new economic reality. Munstead Wood and Jekyll's other gardens helped to redefine "Englishness", both at home and abroad.

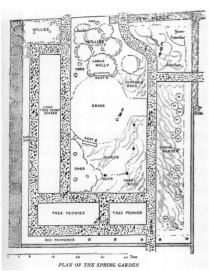

PLAN OF THE SPRING GARDEN

Great Dixter

Created by a father but made famous by his son, this dynamic garden has long been a key player in the development of garden fashions.

Wealthy printing firm owner Nathaniel Lloyd bought Dixter, a 15th-century manor house near Rye in East Sussex, in 1909, and set about transforming it into a country pile that matched his aspirations. He engaged renowned Arts and Crafts architect Edwin Lutyens to combine the existing house with that of a similar timber-framed hall, which was moved, piece by piece, from Benenden in Kent. With the addition of a two-storey building in red brick and tile to unite the two, Great Dixter was born.

Lloyd and Lutyens then turned their attention to the grounds. Although Lutyens often partnered with master horticulturalist Gertrude Jekyll to meld country houses with ground-breaking gardens, on this occasion, he worked alone. It is his structure that endures today, with its trademark York sandstone paving and extensive use of tiles. Lloyd, meanwhile, took charge of the hedging and topiary that would later prove so integral to the garden's planting.

In full bloom

It is Nathaniel Lloyd's charismatic youngest son, Christopher, who turned Great Dixter into one of England's most influential gardens. A celebrated gardener and garden writer, Christopher – or "Christo" – made the house his lifelong home, and wrote regular articles describing his enthusiasm for plants and planting and his experiments with the use of colour, texture, and exotic plants.

The garden now consists of many elements, which surround the house to create a sometimes overwhelming horticultural experience. The Front Meadow, rich with orchids, fritillaries, and other spring meadow flowers, softens the approach to the front entrance, and this style of planting continues in

above *Topiary in the Peacock Garden;* **right** *Christopher Lloyd with Fergus Garrett, who has been head gardener at Great Dixter since 1993*

*The Exotic Garden, filled with vibrant colours
from the cannas, dahlias, and verbenas, and the
hardy Japanese banana plant,* Musa bajoo

the Orchard. Separated from the meadow by a York stone path, the dynamic Long Border blooms almost continually for six months of the year. Trees, flowers, grasses, climbers, and shrubs combine to create the illusion of informal planting against a formal backdrop of topiary arches. One of these archways leads to the High Garden, a kitchen garden and plant nursery that affords excellent views of the house.

Nathaniel Lloyd created the structure of the Sunk Garden and Barn Garden, while his son designed the planting. Nathaniel's love of topiary (a recurrent feature in Arts and Crafts gardens) is showcased in the Topiary Lawn and Peacock Garden, albeit not quite on its former scale – the 18 topiary pheasants, blackbirds, and suchlike in the latter garden have now all more or less morphed into peacocks.

Trendsetter
Great Dixter has long been at the forefront of gardening trends – Christopher caused a major controversy when he dug out Lutyens' highly regarded formal rose garden and replaced it with the Exotic Garden. The bold colours and extravagant foliage of this tropical space peak in late summer and early autumn, and have inspired a widespread fashion for exotics.

Christopher would often discuss his development of new garden styles with his lifelong friend and correspondent, the legendary plantswoman Beth Chatto, and, like her, he was most likely influenced by Cedric Morris's outstanding gardens at Benton End (see p.122). Since Christopher's death in 2006, Great Dixter has been managed by the Great Dixter Charitable Trust, under whose care this ground-breaking garden continues to evolve.

Women emerge: Suffragette Woods

"The idea of a field of trees grows."

Emily Blathwayt, writing in her diary, 28 April 1909

As the 20th century loomed, the suffragette movement in the UK gained momentum, backed by many strong and pioneering horticultural women. Gertrude Jekyll was a prominent campaigner, even working on and contributing to the marching banner for the Godalming branch of the National Union of Women's Suffrage Societies (NUWSS). Her close friend Mrs C.W. Earle, a well-known gardening writer, was also involved – perhaps inevitably so since Earle was aunt to the influential activist Constance Lytton and her sister Emily (wife of the architect Edwin Lutyens). With these connections, it seems fitting that one of the representations of women's suffrage should be horticultural, in the form of Suffragette Wood, also known as Annie's Arboretum.

Eagle House in Batheaston, near Bath, was an unassuming country house owned by Lieutenant-Colonel Linley Wynter Blathwayt. Linley's wife, Emily, was a suffragette and an active – though non-militant – member of the Women's Social and Political Union (WSPU), which was founded by Emmeline Pankhurst and others in 1903. Frustrated by the treatment of suffragettes, many of whom had been disowned by their families and faced destitution, the Blathwayt family decided to offer them a place of refuge.

Linley, Emily, and their daughter, Mary, built a summerhouse in the extensive grounds of Eagle House to provide sanctuary for activists. Hearing tales of the unimaginable horror these women had faced in prison inspired the Blathwayts to memorialize the suffragettes' struggle.

Between 1909 and 1912 more than 50 trees were individually planted within the 2-acre site that ran along the side of Solsbury Hill. The Blathwayts created a record of each one: Linley, a budding amateur photographer, would capture the suffragettes posed by their trees, and Mary and Emily, both tireless diarists, would note down the date and who planted which tree. Each one was then marked by a lead plaque. Among the names recorded were Emmeline Pankhurst, Christabel Pankhurst, Millicent Fawcett, Constance Lytton, and Annie Kenney.

Annie's Arboretum

Annie Kenney, who had moved to Bristol after being appointed WSPU organizer for the West of England, met Mary soon after. The Blathwayts welcomed Kenney, and she stayed at Eagle House most weekends, riding, playing tennis, and relaxing. It is clear from the way they began to refer to the plantation as "Annie's Arboretum" that the family had a great affection for her.

As the suffragette movement became increasingly militant, the Blathwayt family became conflicted about their involvement. Planting at the arboretum continued, but only to honour non-violent members. When the suffragettes' "direct action" escalated to include assaulting the home secretary, Herbert Gladstone, planting a bomb at the home of David Lloyd George, then Chancellor of the Exchequer, and, in 1914, placing a bomb beneath the

Coronation Chair in Westminster Abbey, the Blathwayts could no longer justify their support. Numerous suffragettes were asked not to return to Eagle House.

In 1961, a planning application was made for a section of the grounds at Eagle House to be used to create council housing. Despite recognition of the estate's general heritage, no mention was made of the arboretum or its significance. Today, only one tree still stands (a black pine planted in 1909 by Rose Lamartine Yates), lovingly maintained by a local resident.

Annie Kenney, Mary Blathwayt, and Emmeline Pankhurst planting Cedrus deodara *at Eagle House, 1910*

Artists
and
gardens

"One needs years of patience to make a garden;
one needs deeply to love it..."

Vita Sackville-West, House & Garden, *1950*

Throughout the centuries gardens have been an intriguing subject for art, and many artists in turn have graduated to garden making, not least the main protagonists of the English Landscape Movement, William Kent, Lancelot "Capability" Brown, and Humphry Repton, all of whom began as painters. However, it was only in the 20th century that the two became inextricably linked when the artist-gardener came into being, forming artistic communities and creating gardens as part of their creative ethos.

Charleston

In England it was primarily the Bloomsbury Group who would create their own sanctuary – from the city, from the wars, from the confines of social and sexual convention – in the form of both art and gardens.

Leading the way were artists and lovers Vanessa Bell and Duncan Grant, who settled at Charleston in Sussex in 1916. Over the following five decades the house would play host, often for considerable periods of time, to a plethora of painters, writers, and academics who shared their bohemian ideals, including the writer (and Grant's lover) David Garnett, Bell's husband Clive, economist John Maynard Keynes, novelist E.M. Forster, writer Lytton Strachey, and art critic Roger Fry.

Charleston was not just a home to the group; it would become their canvas, too. Much like at Benton End (see p.122), the residents would decorate every inch of the house's interior, before turning their eye to the walled garden, which was created largely by Bell and Grant, in the fashionable cottage garden style within a semiformal Mediterranean design by Roger Fry. As a follower of William Robinson and Gertrude Jekyll, Grant filled the garden with fragrance, form, and luxuriant colour set against contrasting silver foliage, which would inspire not only him and Bell to paint it, but also "visiting" artists like Dora Carrington. The revolutionary mix of styles fostered a unique and tranquil atmosphere that sparked the artists' creativity.

Garsington Manor

As well as Charleston, numerous other residences became outposts for the group's artistic expression. Bell's sister Virginia Woolf and her husband Leonard lived nearby at Monk's Cottage, with its inspirational cottage garden, while Virginia Woolf's lover Vita Sackville-West was creating her own magnificent garden at Sissinghurst in Kent (see p.118), with her husband Harold Nicolson.

The fine Garsington Manor in Oxfordshire would also play host to the Bloomsbury cognoscenti but told a slightly different story. The house was bought in 1914 by the scandalous Lady Ottoline Morrell and her husband, while the garden was restored in the Italian style by Arts and Crafts disciple Charles Mallows. Perhaps more significant, however, was that in 1916 the Morrells invited conscientious objectors, including Clive Bell and Duncan Grant, to work on Garsington's farm during the war. Food production was considered a valid alternative to military service – making Garsington a political statement as well as an artistic one.

From William Morris's Kelmscott Manor, to Rudyard Kipling's Bateman's, to the Bloomsbury Group's retreats, many artists have found great creative allure in their gardens, with some, such as Gertrude Jekyll, even becoming successful garden designers. For these artists, gardens could be sanctuary, muse, and work of art all in one, the basis and inspiration for a life of peace, creativity, beauty, and freedom.

The Doorway *by Duncan Grant, 1929, capturing a framed snapshot of the garden at Charleston*

Sissinghurst

This world-famous garden is known for its themed garden "rooms" that combine geometric form with informal planting.

The famous White Garden at Sissinghurst, with mulliganii roses scrambling over a central pergola, and white foxgloves and cosmos threaded through box-lined borders

W riter Vita Sackville-West and her husband, diplomat Harold Nicolson, bought Sissinghurst Castle in Kent in 1930. Vita was enchanted by her ancestral links with the place – Thomas Sackville had married the daughter of Sissinghurst's owner, John Baker, in 1554 – and by its peaceful setting. Together, the amateur horticulturalists set about restoring the derelict property and creating one of the most famous gardens in the world.

Rooms with a view

Despite leading very separate lives, Harold and Vita adored each other, and the result of their passionate collaboration is a gloriously romantic garden bursting with joie de vivre. It is made up of a series of outdoor "rooms", with the structure ("walls" and "windows") provided by Harold, and the planting ("furnishings") curated by Vita.

The White Garden is the stuff of horticultural legend. It began its life as a rose garden, but developed into what Vita called the "pale garden" in the 1950s. The couple used only white, green, grey, and silver plants, enclosed within yew and box hedging, to create the restrained effect we see today. The South Cottage Garden, by contrast, is exuberant and brightly coloured. This is the rousing view that the couple would wake up to each morning.

Both Vita's and Harold's touch is again evident in the newer Rose Garden, with its "tumble of roses and honeysuckle, figs and vines" (in Vita's words) and the Rondel, a circular hedge that reflects Harold's military precision and love of geometric shapes. In the Orchard, however, formality is thrown aside and wildness prevails. Hidden paths are mown through tall grasses interspersed with meadow flowers, and roses tumble from apple trees. In the furthest corner stands a gazebo, built in memory of Harold in 1969. This unusual building looks outwards from the moat

right *The Rose Garden's circular yew hedge;* **far right** *Wallflowers, tulips, and euphorbias in the warm South Cottage Garden;* **below** *The Delos Garden, a modern re-creation of Vita and Harold's vision of a holiday-inspired Mediterranean garden*

onto the Kent countryside, where the ornamental farm planting (an interpretation by grandson Adam Nicolson and his wife, gardener Sarah Raven, of the farming practices used originally at Sissinghurst) bridges the gap between the garden and its surrounding landscape.

Mediterranean vibe

After visiting the Greek island of Delos in 1935, Vita and Harold sought to replicate its Mediterranean atmosphere at home but were foiled by the damp climate of Kent and the heavy clay soil.

However, Vita's romantic vision of a garden where ruins were "smothered…by mats of the wild flowers of Greece" has now been masterfully reimagined by head gardener Troy Scott Smith and designer Dan Pearson. In the Delos Garden, they have introduced more robust plant strains, used columns to create the feel of ancient Greek ruins, and reoriented the area so it faces south. Raised beds filled with gravel and a lighter, well-draining soil mix also help the Mediterranean plants to thrive.

Delos is a wonderful addition and illustrates how Vita and Harold continue to influence the garden's development from beyond the grave.

Benton End

For many artists, gardening and painting are two sides of the same creative process. At this creative hub and home, Sir Cedric Morris would be the only one of his generation to achieve national recognition for both.

At Benton End, a gloriously attractive 16th-century "Suffolk Pink" farmhouse, Cedric Morris beautifully interwove his twin passions for art and horticulture. Morris, with his lifelong partner and fellow painter Arthur Lett-Haines, established the East Anglian School of Painting and Drawing, which they ran at Benton End from 1939 after a fire destroyed their previous premises in Dedham. Over the years, visitors and students would include the elite among their artistic contemporaries – Frances Hodgkins, Barbara Hepworth, Joan Warburton, Lucian Freud, and Maggi Hambling – forming a bohemian community not unlike that of the Bloomsbury Group at Charleston in Sussex (see p.116). Within the house, blushing pink-washed walls were hung with vivid botanical and landscape paintings, while the garden would become Morris's paradise, profuse with colours and textures expressing his painterly eye, which would inspire his students' art and his own.

Exotic paradise

The emphasis throughout the garden was towards the highly exotic, with a vibrant collection of flowers from the many plants Morris gathered on his trips abroad, mainly in the Mediterranean and North Africa. A favourite was *Zauschneria californica* susp. *cana* 'Sir Cedric Morris', a vivid vermilion fuschia-like plant with trumpet-shaped flowers collected by Morris on his travels to Mexico. He would return from successful plant-hunting trips to Portugal with the all-white rock rose *Cistus palhinhae*, and from Spain with the much-prized Narcissus minor 'Cedric Morris', an early-flowering dwarf daffodil gathered from a roadside by plant hunter Basil Leng, which Morris grew on and passed on to Beth Chatto, who would register the daffodil in Morris's name. Morris also bred 90 new iris cultivars, growing up to 1,000 iris seedlings each year, which delighted visitors with their breadth of colour and which he saw as an extension of his art. Vita Sackville-West coveted these irises and benefited from many gifts from Morris, which grow to this day at Sissinghurst (see p.118).

Beth Chatto, Morris's protégée, affectionately described Benton End as a "bewildering, mind-stretching, eye-widening canvas of colour, textures and shapes"; she would continue Morris's legacy both through her cultivation of his plants and in his wild, loose, natural gardening style. However, it was the arrival of plantsman Nigel Scott during the 1950s that would focus Morris's ambitions for the garden. He and Scott, who also became his lover, worked tirelessly to expand the planting and take the garden to its magnificent colourful peak. Morris would even name one of his most famous irises after him – the 'Benton Nigel'.

Regeneration

Writer Ronald Blythe vividly recalled Benton End as "a paradise of pollen and paint", full of students with their easels nestled within the colourful beds of poppies and irises. Though currently closed to visitors, the site has recently been acquired by London's Garden Museum, which aims to develop a public garden that shares the spirit, values, and ethos of Cedric Morris and his partner Arthur Lett-Haines. It will be beautifully planted to include plants Morris grew and cultivated, celebrating his contribution to horticulture, and firmly establishing his significance as both an artist and a gardener.

top *Benton End today, with Morris's beloved irises making a return as part of the garden's revival;* **above** May Flowering Irises No.2 *by Cedric Morris, 1935*

Women help each other

"Adequate education … is what the agricultural labourer now needs most of all."

Daisy Greville, Joseph Arch: The Story of his Life, *1898*

Until the 20th century women were rarely employed in gardens, and even when they were it was usually as "women weeders", carrying out back-breaking manual work that was poorly paid. This was largely due to the lack of horticultural training for women – one of the many areas of education they had historically been excluded from – and so, recognizing this, women began to help each other, and themselves, to resolve the issue.

Women writers

A breakthrough came in the mid 19th century with Jane Loudon, who worked closely with her husband, parks and gardens genius John Claudius Loudon, and studied botany, attending lectures by John Lindley. It was out of necessity that Jane turned to writing to supplement the family income; her first book, *Young Lady's Book of Botany*, published in 1838, was one of several practical gardening books specifically aimed at middle-class women that she would write throughout the 1840s and 1850s, which were very successful. All of her works encouraged women to venture into their gardens and create ornamental displays, and to produce fruit and vegetables for the family, opening their eyes to the potential in their gardens and in themselves.

Jane Loudon died in 1858, but she had inspired a whole host of women garden writers, including Louisa Johnson,

Studley Castle Horticultural College for Women · A lesson in Pruning

whose books assumed little horticultural knowledge and opened up a whole new world to the amateur lady gardener, including the joys of taking cuttings, potting up, and showing plants at flower shows. Edith Chamberlain's *The Gentlewoman's Book of Gardening*, published in 1892, still assumed its readers' amateur status, but in fact the garden industry was becoming increasingly open to the participation of women.

The rise of women's colleges

The first step towards enabling women to become professional gardeners was the introduction of dedicated women's colleges. The first of these was Swanley Horticultural College in Kent, though it began in 1889 offering courses only to men; within five years, however, after trials were held to reassure the college board that women could withstand the rigours of such a physically demanding occupation, the college took the ground-breaking decision to be exclusively for women. Swanley offered both practical and theoretical teaching; women were expected to work in the gardens, but also to attend lectures in the laboratories, on subjects ranging from botany to beekeeping to garden design. In 1904 Fanny Wilkinson – who already held the accolade of being England's first female landscape designer and would create over 75 public gardens throughout her career – was appointed its first female principal.

Students taking part in a pruning lesson at Studley Horticultural and Agricultural College for Women, in 1910; the college was established by Daisy Greville, Countess of Warwick, in 1898

The success of Swanley inspired the opening of many other women's colleges; it is estimated that 20 were established between 1894 and the beginning of the Second World War. Hot on the trail was Studley Horticultural and Agricultural College for Women, created by the formidable Daisy Greville, Countess of Warwick – active campaigner for female emancipation and an early convert to socialism despite her upper-class status. Further examples include Thatcham Fruit and Flower Farm in Berkshire, and the Waterperry School of Horticulture in Oxfordshire, created by the indomitable Beatrix Havergal.

Beatrix Havergal, the founder and principal of Waterperry School of Horticulture in Oxfordshire, photographed by Cecil Beaton in 1943

Perhaps the most revolutionary, however, was Duxhurst Industrial Farm Colony in Surrey. Founded in 1895 by Lady Henry Somerset (one of the most famous women of her era, now largely unknown), this residential centre was established for the care of women suffering from alcoholism. The colony was geared towards helping in-patients regain their independence; as well as taking care of the cleaning and laundry, the women were educated in gardening, with fruit growing, beekeeping, and poultry management all encouraged. Their training in agricultural techniques gave them not only the benefits of fresh air and exercise, but also the skills to re-establish themselves in society and obtain employment. It proved highly effective: in the first two years, 55 out of 112 admissions were released a year later, apparently cured, with none returning – a remarkable example of women helping other women with care and success.

The path was finally clear for all kinds of women to forge careers in gardening, and they were ready to step up when opportunity knocked – not least during the two world wars. In 1915, when male employees had gone off to fight, Kew Gardens Curator William Watson was quick to defend the 15 women he had employed directly from the horticultural colleges, stating that they were undoubtedly equal to their male counterparts. Meanwhile, the Women's Agricultural and Horticultural International Union, formed in 1899 – of which Fanny Wilkinson was a founder member – would be key in establishing the Women's Land Army, first in 1917, and then again in 1939, to help with food production and land maintenance during wartime. New possibilities in horticulture had opened up for women, and many of them would never look back.

BEATRIX HAVERGAL
1901–1980

Known as "Miss H" to her students, Beatrix Havergal sought to combat the challenges for women gardeners by establishing her own horticultural college for ladies at Waterperry House in Oxfordshire. She and her partner, Avice Sanders, welcomed students first at their cottage at Pusey House in 1927, and then at Waterperry in 1932. Their curriculum was radical for the time, consisting of "a theoretical and thoroughly practical training". Havergal received an MBE and numerous RHS medals in recognition of her work, and though the school closed in 1971, Waterperry remains a magnificent garden. Havergal's legacy also lives on in the achievements of her students and, affectionately, in the character Miss Trunchbull in Roald Dahl's *Matilda*, whose stature and dress sense (though nothing else!) she inspired.

Flower shows

"I never yet saw flower gardening carried on in such high order."

Donald Beaton, writing on Kensington's nascent museum quarter in the Journal of Horticulture, *1861*

While there have been flower shows of a sort recorded in England since the 17th century, they were not what we might recognize as such today. These early incarnations were known as "florists' feasts" and were usually organized in a local public house, with awards being given to amateur flower growers during the dinner that followed the competition. It was not until 1804, when the Horticultural Society was first founded, that the story of flower shows as we know them began to take shape.

The first flower shows

Chiswick was home to the Horticultural Society's garden, and it was here that they held their first formal show in 1827. A few years later, in 1832, the rival Metropolitan Society of Florists and Amateurs was founded, and, as is often the case, each society's show attempted to outdo the other. Recognizing the commercial potential, others soon entered the fray: first the Royal Botanic Society, which in 1840 began its flower show within the Inner Circle of Regent's Park, and then the Crystal Palace Company, which opened its show in its own grounds in 1855.

This rapid growth in flower shows led the Horticultural Society, by now the London Horticultural Society, to establish a new garden in Kensington's nascent museum quarter, as Chiswick was then poorly served by the railway network. With this magnificent garden – which was a big-budget affair, designed by landscape architect William Andrews Nesfield and overseen by Prince Albert himself, with pillared arcades, fountains, and canals aplenty, and a grand glasshouse at its centre – the society soon re-established its dominance and earned royal patronage from Queen Victoria when it opened in 1861. The newly minted Royal Horticultural Society would hold its first "Great Spring Show" the following year.

The RHS Chelsea Flower Show

The Spring Show – now known the world over as the Chelsea Flower Show – continued at Kensington until 1888; after a brief stint at Temple Gardens, the show was again in need of a new site, when Harry Veitch, latest owner of England's largest nursery (see p.87), managed to lease the grounds of the Royal Hospital Chelsea. The show was held there for the first time in 1913, and it was such a success that it has been held there nearly every year since. The Chelsea Flower Show as we know it had been born.

Following the ground-breaking botanical work and the plant-hunting expeditions of the 19th century, England, and particularly London, was by now a major centre for horticultural expertise. What had begun as a show held in one tent had grown to several, and in the 1920s Chelsea expanded its offering even further to include the very first show gardens, as well as specialist tents (for roses, for example), scientific displays, and garden design exhibits. It was also during the interwar period that the show first became something of a high-society event, with celebrities, aristocrats, and royalty making regular appearances.

During the 1930s many of the traditions we now associate with Chelsea were first established, such as medals day on the Tuesday, and a royal visit. The Second World War stopped the show in its tracks, however, and its return afterwards was by no means immediate. In the aftermath of the war plant stocks were low, staff numbers were much reduced, and the RHS's focus had for several years been diverted to its Dig for Victory campaign, encouraging people to grow their own fruit and vegetables at home. Despite the doubters, the RHS felt strongly that

Watercolour of the Horticultural Gardens in South Kensington, by William Leighton Leitch, 1861. The project was overseen by Prince Albert, who became president of the Horticultural Society in 1858 and opened the gardens in June 1861, shortly before his death

Chelsea should resume in 1947, and although the displays were not what they once were, the show was a great success, and even had an unexpected benefit – it marked the introduction of flower arrangements to make up for the plant shortfall. The Chelsea Flower Show would not be so disrupted again until the onset of the global Covid-19 pandemic in 2020.

From the 1950s to the 1980s, in the postwar era of aspirational living and home improvement, it was boom time for the flower shows – hundreds of professional exhibitors displayed at scores of shows every year, drawing many thousands of visitors. And although today it is harder for the smaller independent shows to flourish, the big RHS shows – Chelsea and Hampton Court Palace in London, and Tatton Park in Cheshire – remain big business, and a staple of the spring and summer gardening year. Vast and spectacular, the flower show today is a grand day out, a place to be inspired and find unusual plants, and a stage set for designers to show off their skills and compete for coveted medals.

Commercial floristry

Though homegrown flowers have for centuries been used to decorate our homes, the creation of floristry as a commercial business was a 19th-century development. With the introduction of new cut-flower species from all over the world, improved hothouse design, and expanding travel networks, the wholesale flower trade flourished – so much so that the magnificent ironwork Flower Hall was built in 1860 at Covent Garden to house a vast new flower market. Floral arrangements for weddings, bouquets, table decorations, and funerals were in high demand in Victorian Britain, and designed according to the formal, opulent, showy style of the era.

Constance Spry

It was a former headmistress who would drive a truck through the uptight rules of Victorian flower arranging. Constance Spry was without question the most influential floral decorator of the 20th century. Throwing off tradition, her revolutionary floral designs explored a

An all-pink arrangement of roses and carnations by Constance Spry, from December 1951, referencing the 1675 painting Group of Flowers *by Dutch artist Willem van Aelst*

natural, seasonal vision, introducing unusual plant materials to offset her flowers, such as pussy willow, weeds, grasses, bark, seed heads, and even ornamental kale and rhubarb leaves, which was entirely modern. She was also known for rummaging in friends' attics to gather items for her displays, from wicker bicycle baskets to old cooking tins.

Spry was not just a creative force; she was also a highly successful entrepreneur. In 1929 she opened her first shop, Flower Decoration, in Pimlico, and her second, larger one in Mayfair in 1934. Spry was now at the peak of her career; over the years she would publish more than a dozen books, develop her own range of flower vases, and establish the Constance Spry Flower School at her new premises. In 1938, a lecture tour in the US even led to an invitation to open a store in New York.

Such flair was reflected in her private life, too, which was worthy of a Hollywood movie. Belying her prim appearance, Spry had an array of interesting lovers, including the gender-nonconformist artist Gluck, and was part of a circle of luminaries, including photographer Sir Cecil Beaton, interior designer Syrie Maugham, fashion designer Norman Hartnell, artist Rex Whistler, and actor Greta Garbo. With such friends and clients, Spry quickly became the go-to floral artist for society weddings and parties, with the press coverage to match (*Vogue* was always a great supporter). Spry's illustrious commissions included the 1937 wedding

of Wallis Simpson and the Duke of Windsor and the Coronation of Queen Elizabeth II in 1953.

As a great modernizer, a pioneering businesswoman, and an unconventional spirit, Constance Spry is an inspirational figure in step with our own time, and her influence continues to be felt in modern floristry. Her naturalistic, minimalist style, her use of quirky, alternative "vases", and her penchant for single-colour – often all-white – arrangements are much referenced by today's floral designers and look perfectly at home in contemporary spaces. The resurgence of interest in her work extends even to educating the next generation. To quote Wagner Kreusch, Managing Director of the London Flower School, who teaches courses dedicated to Spry: "[her] work remains as fresh today as it ever was."

Constance Spry at work on an arrangement for fashion designer Hardy Amies, 1960

it's not

all

country

"Suppose people lived in little communities among gardens and
green fields ... one might hope civilisation had really begun."

William Morris, Letter to Louie Baldwin, 1874

life

Garden cities

"How to restore the people to the land – that beautiful land of ours..."

Ebenezer Howard, Garden Cities of To-Morrow, *1898*

With industrialization on the increase and over half the population (and counting) living in a city by the mid 19th century, England faced mounting social, economic, and environmental problems that would dominate architecture and landscape planning for decades. An attempt to resolve such issues as overpopulated slums and poverty, the Garden City Movement was one of England's most radical chapters in urban design.

The idea came from the 1898 book *Garden Cities of To-Morrow* by urban planner Ebenezer Howard. His utopian vision was for a lush, green garden city full of employment opportunities and modern houses with their own sizeable garden plot, allowing every resident to experience the "joyous union" between town and country.

The garden city vision

Howard was inspired by the Arts and Crafts Movement (see p.102), and the model villages of Bournville outside Birmingham, created by the Cadbury family, and Port Sunlight on the Wirral, built by Lever Brothers, to accommodate their factory employees. Both had been resounding successes, providing modern homes with gardens, green spaces, free sports facilities, community halls, and healthcare – everything any resident could need apart from a pub!

His vision was based upon the "Three Magnet" principle, whereby the garden city was the "third magnet" that combined the pull of country living and of city living, creating a better quality of life for all.

The proposed blueprint was circular: at the centre there would be a park surrounded by public buildings. Howard envisaged crescents and terraces spread along this broad, circular "Grand Avenue", with central grassed areas containing schools and churches. Each garden city would be as self-sufficient as possible and limited to 32,000 residents. The concept

GARDEN·CITY·
BALDOCK ROAD
LETCHWORTH.

received much praise, with dissent largely coming from Howard's friend, playwright George Bernard Shaw, and the socialist Fabian Society, who thought it overly simplistic. Shaw at least would soon be on board, however; he became an investor in the very first project.

The first garden city

Building began on the first garden city, Letchworth in Hertfordshire, in 1903. Architects Barry Parker and Raymond Unwin had won the commission and now it was time for theory and plan to come together. Houses were inspired by the architecture of Edwin Lutyens and Charles Voysey, though they varied in size, shape, and style, while the gardens also followed Arts and Crafts fashion, with Gertrude Jekyll-style borders. Unlike Howard's plan, the city's layout was not a perfect circle, but more organic, with houses grouped around a green, following the traditional village concept, though generously spaced at 12 per acre.

Despite these nods to informality, there were plenty of rules for keeping the city looking immaculate. Each garden was fronted by a hedge, and it was part of the tenancy agreement that this would be maintained to a regular height. Front lawns were to be mown most weeks and no alterations, including ponds, sheds, tree planting, and hard landscaping, were allowed until permission had been granted – a stipulation that still stands. Even hanging out washing on a Sunday was forbidden! The utopian vision had to be maintained.

Grand houses on Baldock Road in newly built Letchworth Garden City, Hertfordshire

Garden cities blossom

The garden city formula proved appealing and would go on to influence the further developments of Hampstead Garden Suburb in 1907 and Welwyn Garden City in 1920.

Welwyn followed the style of Letchworth, though on a far larger scale, with a central boulevard over a mile long. The architect, Louis de Soissons, grouped buildings for visual impact and experimented with cul-de-sac design, but, as Howard had specified at Letchworth, there were no more than 12 houses to an acre. The variety in building style was ensured by employing over 20 different architects, but every design was overseen by De Soissons and the overall appearance was one of unity and Englishness.

One deviation from the original Howard concept was shifting the style of front garden from hedged to open – a style De Soissons possibly brought over from Canada. Furthermore, before building began, the position of every tree on the original land – mainly oaks and elms – was recorded and the new city cleverly incorporated them. In the spirit of the urban garden they were creating, few trees were cut down where possible, while roads were planted with new ones. And in every garden, an apple tree was planted by Ebenezer Howard himself.

Letchworth and Welwyn garden cities served as successful prototypes that were much copied, both in Britain and even more so internationally, throughout the 20th century. In more recent years, garden cities have attracted criticism as agents of urban sprawl that ultimately damage rather than bolster the environment and economy, but versions of them are still

> " By so laying out a Garden City that, as it grows, the free gifts of Nature – fresh air, sunlight, breathing room and playing room – shall be still retained in all needed abundance… "

Ebenezer Howard, Garden Cities of To-Morrow, *1898*

proposed by modern-day governments as a solution to our housing crisis.

The rise of suburbia

Encroachment of suburban sprawl throughout England triggered a dramatic change in gardening during the 20th century. Before then, the focus of garden and landscape design had been on the vast estates of the landed gentry; ordinary folk were sometimes allowed to visit, but wonderful gardens were always something they could only admire from the other side of the ha-ha. However, with the rise of garden cities and suburban housing estates came sizeable garden plots. The masses now had an opportunity to express themselves through their own plant and design choices – the democratization of gardening had arrived.

Between the two world wars, a succession of housing acts were passed by the UK government to address the shortage of low-cost housing for working-class people and to offer local councils subsidies to clear poverty-stricken slums and rehouse their inhabitants. The first was the Housing and Town Planning Act of 1919, or the Addison Act – an attempt to make good on Prime Minister David Lloyd George's 1918 election promise of building homes "fit for heroes". The Tudor Walters Report of 1918 had set the standards for council house design: short terraces of three-bedroom houses, 12 per acre, with fitted bathrooms and kitchens, and each with their own garden. And although the government didn't reach its promised quota, by 1939 1.1 million council houses, plus 2.8 million middle-class homes, had been built, transforming England from the most urbanized country in the world to the most suburbanized in just 20 years.

The aspirational look of this new suburbia was typified by a band of urbanized countryside just northwest of London, which would be dubbed Metro-land, a term coined in 1915 by the Metropolitan Railway to promote the area as a country idyll that was within easy reach of the city. The posters presented the endless avenues of semidetached mock-Tudor villas, with their steep roofs, bay windows, half-timbered gables, and immaculate front gardens, as the ultimate image of desirable living. The Metropolitan Railway's PR department had invented the English suburban dream through their evocative advertising and everyone wanted more.

Status and aspiration

British Railways carriage print advertising Welwyn Garden City in the 1950s, based on a painting by George Henry Stringer

The tenancy agreements of these new council houses made it clear that householders were expected to meet and maintain this idealized vision of suburban England. The rules stated that front gardens should be kept neat and tidy, not just for aesthetic reasons, but because a well-tended garden was considered a marker of respectability.

In imitation of country-house gardens, herbaceous borders surrounding manicured striped lawns with a bird bath at the centre, all tucked behind perfectly trimmed privet hedges or picket fences, were considered the height of good taste, but some reacted against this uniformity with individual expression. Garden gnomes and crazy paving became strong themes in suburbia, as did patriotic red, white, and blue carpet bedding. The suburban garden became a battleground for class snobbery. The gaudy and vulgar was looked down upon, and if gardens weren't maintained to regulation standards the rent collector would soon tick tenants off. There were even awards for the Best Kept Garden. Suddenly gardens were a showcase, reflecting the social status and aspirations of an entire generation. The pressure was on to get it right.

Woolworths: England's garden centre

First and foremost, enthusiastic suburban gardeners needed a convenient, affordable place to purchase supplies. Nurseries were expensive, and before the advent of garden centres in the mid 1950s Woolworths was the place to go. From 1910 well into the 1980s, the high-street chain was the UK's mainstream retailer of plants, seeds, and bulbs – which it cleverly sold in an open display like its pick-'n'-mix of sweets – with over 500 stores across the country. Indeed, it's estimated that at least one in three of the daffodils we see in spring were originally from Woolworths.

The store met every DIY gardener's needs: it sold tools, compost, lawnmowers, even flat-pack sheds and picket fencing (a bestseller at sixpence a yard); it produced leaflets full of advice and encouraged gardeners to grow vegetables during the wartime Dig for Victory campaign. To complete the aspirational picture, it would win multiple gold medals for its gardens at the RHS Chelsea Flower Show and even have two roses named in its honour – 'Chelsea Gold' and 'Wonder of Woolies' – both instant successes!

Woolworths' dominance dwindled as garden centres, supermarkets, and DIY giants tempted a large proportion of its customers away, and the shift to online retail was the final death blow. But for decades a horticultural revolution was conducted from the front counter at Woolworths, backed up by its famous guarantee: "Success or your money back!"

A Woolworths gardening leaflet from the 1950s, which featured advice from popular gardening broadcaster Fred Streeter

New media and suburban inspiration

The owners of the first suburban gardens in the early 20th century were thrilled with their new plots, but then the reality hit them: what should they do with them? What style, plants, and layout should they use? What were the neighbours up to? Garden magazines, books and, of course, the growth in garden tourism, aided by the expanding railway network and the boom in car ownership, helped them grapple with these decisions, but it was the new media of radio and television that would bring suburban gardeners what they needed most: some friendly advice.

Radio days

The BBC started broadcasting gardening talks as early as 1922, the very year it was founded, but the first gardening radio programme, *The Week in the Garden*, was broadcast on 9 May 1931. It took the form of a series of 15-minute talks, presented by Cecil Henry Middleton, or "Mr Middleton" as he became known, a knowledgeable gardener who had been recommended by the RHS. His relaxed, conversational tone and practical tips were a welcome change from the clipped tones and scripted monologues of most early BBC presenters, and it made him a huge hit with audiences.

The programme soon developed to become *In Your Garden* and was moved to a prime radio slot on Sunday afternoons, where it attracted 3.5 million listeners. The programme's success would establish BBC radio, rather than any newspaper or magazine, as the leading source of gardening information for the public – a tradition that *Gardeners' Question Time*, which began life as *How Does Your Garden Grow?* on the Northern network in 1947, continues to this day.

On the small screen

When the BBC launched its television service in 1936, Mr Middleton was the natural choice to bring *In Your Garden* to the small screen, and the following year a garden was purpose-built at Alexandra Palace for him to host the show from. Before both horticultural shows and television itself were cancelled during the Second World War, Middleton also presented the first broadcasts from the Chelsea Flower Show – another ground-breaking hit that allowed many suburban gardeners access to a show they had likely never attended, though only in black and

---

MARGERY FISH

1892–1969

Margery Fish was a gardener and writer who had a great influence on mid-century home-gardening style. In 1937, she and her husband Walter bought East Lambrook Manor in Somerset but disagreed vehemently on the style they wanted for the garden; Margery preferred an informal cottage garden, Walter a formal layout. Only after Walter's death in 1947 would she finally get her way. What Margery created was an iconic cottage garden but on a domestic scale. It didn't require a whole team of gardeners; this was gardening accessible to all. Genial, passionate, and above all relatable, Margery wrote numerous books and magazine articles, and even made guest appearances on BBC radio, explaining the right plants and techniques to use. She became the go-to source for middle-class gardeners seeking advice on maintaining their own small private gardens, and her style of mixing "old-fashioned" and contemporary perennials remains with us.

white, of course. During the war Middleton also did his bit for the Dig for Victory campaign, a trusted voice encouraging his audience to sacrifice flowers for vegetables and utilize any scrap of land they could find for the good of the nation.

In 1945, however, just as the war was ending, Middleton died suddenly. When television resumed after the war, new faces took over as the nation's gardening gurus, most notably Fred Streeter, head gardener at Petworth, who became Mr Middleton's successor and was said to be impossible to dislike, and the mild-mannered Percy Thrower, who from 1955 until 1967 hosted *Gardening Club* from a rooftop garden set at Lime Grove Studios.

In colour

The demise of *Gardening Club* made way for a new programme, also presented by Percy Thrower, which for the first time would bring the glory of plants into viewers' homes in full colour. The first episode of *Gardeners' World* aired on BBC Two on 5 January 1968, hosted from the Oxford Botanic Garden and billed as "a weekly series for gardeners, advanced and beginners, throughout the British Isles".

Then, as now, the show offered a winning combination of friendly, practical advice, knowledgeable experts, garden visits, and features on garden design and history. Thrower cemented his role as "the nation's head gardener", and brought in the new tradition of presenting the programme from his own garden. Now, over half a century later, it remains a much-loved formula, bringing relaxation, joy, and inspiration to gardeners not just in the British Isles, but all over the world.

Percy Thrower, a staple of TV gardening programmes from the 1950s to the 1970s, in his greenhouse at home in 1966

Modernity and transition

"A modern formula for a practical intake of fresh air"

Le Corbusier, Précisions sur un état présent de l'architecture et de l'urbanisme, *1930*

In the aftermath of the First World War, Europe sought to remake the world in a glorious futuristic movement that would unite all the arts together, without class barriers. In the broad church that would become Modernism, everyone was welcome, with influences ranging from the Bauhaus school in Germany, founded in 1919, to the *De Stijl* ("The Style") movement in the Netherlands, established in 1922. Yet despite its prescriptive design principles regarding everything from architecture to jewellery, Modernism was slow to provide any directive on gardens.

The first Modernist garden

Indeed, it was not until 1925, at the Exposition Internationale des Arts Décoratifs et Industriels Modernes in Paris, that a new garden aesthetic for the machine age emerged. It was here that architect Le Corbusier caused a stir with his first Modernist house design, *Pavillon de l'Esprit Nouveau*, and here that the first Modernist gardens were unveiled.

The most influential of these was the *Jardin d'Eau et de Lumière* ("Garden of Water and Light"), designed by Gabriel Guevrekian. Intended to be viewed only from the outside, the triangular walled space made of concrete and coloured glass, with its Persian influences and triangular flowerbeds in blocks of blue, yellow, and red, was powerful indeed. Central to the garden was a series of geometric tiered pools, on top of which Guevrekian installed a revolving disco-ball-like sculpture by glass artist Louis Barillet, which emitted light that bounced off the reflective surfaces. The garden was one of the most talked-about installations in the exhibition and would ultimately win Guevrekian the Grand Prix. The Modernist garden had arrived in style.

English Modernism

Despite its flying start in Europe, Modernism seemed reluctant to cross the Channel, with traditional English designers such as Sir Reginald Blomfield and Thomas Mawson vehemently attacking it. Even during the postwar building boom, the style was not popular, and when the first Modernist houses in England did appear – New Ways in Northampton, built in 1926 by Peter Behrens, and High and Over in Amersham, in 1929 by Amyas Connell – there was little consideration for the gardens. Often, they resembled a Gertrude Jekyll design, which looked ridiculous against the crisp, stark lines of the architecture.

The shift came with landscape architect Christopher Tunnard's design for Bentley Wood in Sussex in 1938. Tunnard created a stunning naturalistic setting for the house – one of the most significant of the period, by Serge Chermayeff – that was minimalist, bold, and undeniably modern. An angular terrace terminated in a grid screen and a Henry Moore sculpture, while the surrounding woodland was curated to give open, informal views that flowed into the broader countryside and was planted extensively with daffodils.

In his 1938 book *Gardens in the Modern Landscape*, Tunnard had argued for a return to "Functionalism" in gardens; to consider the garden's use and avoid

Bentley Wood's terrace, photographed in 1938, with Henry Moore's stone Recumbent Figure *(1938) looking out towards the Sussex countryside*

unnecessary decoration. The transition had now begun, but unfortunately for England, at the outbreak of the Second World War Tunnard moved to America and began teaching at Harvard. There, however, his ideas galvanized a whole new generation of designers, who hailed him as the father of the Modernist garden.

Modern urban planning: women take the lead

With the modern postwar era came a necessity for new architecture – power stations, reservoirs, universities, even towns – meaning much of the industrial and urban landscape had to be redeveloped. Leading the charge in this new phase for urban planning was a formidable group of women who have gone largely unrecognized for transforming our public spaces. The story begins at Swanley Horticultural College in Kent (see p.125), where Madeline Agar was one of the first women to complete their landscape design course, in 1895. In 1904 she took over from Fanny Wilkinson as landscape designer for the Metropolitan Public Gardens Association (MPGA), a charity established in 1882 for the preservation of London's parks.

Agar's role would involve creating or redeveloping numerous public gardens, including the Southwark Cathedral Precinct in 1910, the Richardson Evans Memorial Playing Fields in Wimbledon Common in 1921, and the influential Emslie Horniman Pleasance Gardens in Kensington in 1914, which she designed with Charles Voysey as a formal walled garden with oak pergola, moat, and herbaceous planting.

Ever the trailblazer, Agar was also a suffragist, the first woman to publish a practical garden design book in 1911, and a teacher at Swanley, where she inspired a whole new raft of women designers.

One of Agar's most eminent students was Brenda Colvin, who argued that the landscape at large was of greater benefit to humankind than an individual garden. This theory would underpin much of her work and led her to create some of the outstanding public spaces of modern England. Having set up her own practice in 1922, Colvin co-founded the Institute of Landscape Architects in 1929 (later the Landscape Institute), becoming its president in 1951. Of the 300-plus projects she worked on, she focused mainly, at first, on private gardens, but after the war, particularly during the 1950s and 1960s, Colvin turned her attention to industrial sites, such as Trimpley reservoir in Worcestershire, the University of East Anglia campus, and several power stations, including Eggborough. Her sympathy for these landscapes and her innovative solutions to the aesthetic challenges they presented – integrating them into their surroundings with strategic mass plantings – became the standard, bringing greenery, balance, and wildlife to sites that would otherwise have been bleak.

Also a protégé of Madeline Agar at Swanley, Sylvia Crowe was the third towering figure who revolutionized England's postwar landscapes. Crowe became one of the most productive landscape architects of the period. As well as creating numerous gardens for private homes and Oxford colleges, and acting as consultant to the Forestry Commission and Central Electricity Generating Board, she brought the beauty and solace of nature to the most functional and soulless new developments – sites as brutal as Trawsfynydd power station in Wales; the Commonwealth Institute in London; and Harlow New Town in Essex, where Crowe created the extraordinary Water Gardens in 1963, influencing work on all subsequent new towns.

In her writings during the 1950s and 1960s, Crowe articulated her ethos: that with sensitivity and good design, large-scale structures could be accommodated within the landscape without destroying it. It's a lesson all three women absorbed and proved with aplomb.

“Landscaping is often what you leave out, not what you put in. You need absolute simplicity to knit the landscape back again.”

Sylvia Crowe, interview with the New Scientist, *1979*

The Homewood

Patrick Gwynne's first house – his enduring Modernist masterpiece – and its fascinating grounds are a testament to the architect's genius.

The slouching, concrete-and-brick facade of the Homewood, Gwynne's 20th-century villa, set amid woodland gardens

England was particularly resistant to the "less is more" ethos of the early-20th-century Bauhaus school of design. A few Modernist houses were constructed but, with no equivalent landscape design style to accompany them, they tended to be surrounded by the traditional template of lawn encircled by herbaceous borders. This was certainly the case with New Ways, built in Northampton in 1926 by German architect Peter Behrens and dubbed the "first modern house in Britain".

Yet despite its failure to embrace Modernism in the 1930s and 1940s, England saw the rise of two of the movement's most notable landscape architects. The first was Christopher Tunnard, who worked with the architect Serge Chermayeff (co-designer of Bexhill's De La Warr Pavilion) to create the iconic Bentley Wood, near Lewes, East Sussex (see p.143). Tunnard advocated the "functional garden" in his influential Modernist landscape manifesto *Gardens in the Modern Landscape* (1938). The second was Patrick Gwynne, who designed and built the Homewood in Esher, Surrey, in 1938, at the age of 24.

Inspired by renowned architects Le Corbusier and Ludwig Mies van de Rohe, Gwynne designed not only the house, but also the furniture, fittings, and landscape setting. But unlike his Modernist idols, Gwynne emphasized the landscape being arranged for the house rather than the house being built for the existing landscape.

Modernist masterpiece

The Homewood, magnificently perched on pilotis (reinforced columns) and particularly lean in its elevated industrial appearance, was a masterpiece of open-plan living, with a central concrete staircase and areas delineated by a material or colour.

right *Acers flushed with autumn colour, seen from the living room;* below *A curved stepping-stone path stretches across the lily pond, leading visitors on towards the bog garden*

Gwynne lived alone in the house for about 60 years. Both home and workplace, it served as a living portfolio for the architect's potential clients and students. He therefore had time to develop the surrounding landscape. Intended to be a woodland garden rather than a park, the garden celebrates its Surrey context and is a prime example of respecting a garden's "spirit of place" – its unique character. Gwynne curated the existing trees and shrubs while planting silver birches, pines, and firs. Rhododendrons and azaleas added bold colour to the more conventional woodland palette, resulting in a choreographed exuberance. The naturalistic appearance of the garden belies its careful composition, which provides vistas and walks, wonderful eye-catchers, meandering borders, and even a bridge that suddenly appears from a bamboo thicket to cross Gwynne's excavated pond. A stepping-stone path entices the visitor to explore the pond further. The overall effect is of an eloquent variety of colour and texture, ever-changing through the seasons, and endlessly fascinating to view from the vast glass windows of the Homewood.

Gwynne constructed the garden almost as a painting – a backdrop to the house. The eye is drawn with apparently naturalistic planting, with a foreground and middle ground. Yet throughout, there are separate gardens, colour-themed in blues and whites, that surprise and delight as each successive eye-catcher lures the visitor onwards.

Outdoor rooms

"A garden is essentially a place
for use by people..."

John Brookes, Room Outside, *1969*

In the mid 20th century, a mind shift in horticulture transformed the garden from something beautiful to look at into an extension of the house. Not to be confused with that of "garden rooms", the concept of gardens as "outdoor rooms" was as much about lifestyle as it was design. In England, genius landscape designer John Brookes of Denmans fame (see p.152) is hailed as the author of this reinvention. However, to understand what informed his ideas, we must look further afield.

From the Netherlands to California

The influences upon Brookes were multi-pronged. From the Netherlands there was Mien Ruys, who in 1924 began creating experimental small urban gardens at the family nursery, Moerheim, near Dedemsvaart. Her designs were open, simple, clear, often arranged in geometric blocks, often Japanese-inspired, often containing water, architectural planting, or colour-themed borders. Her style was indebted to Modernist art and based upon the socialist principle of creating gardens for the people, and by the 1950s her ideas had great traction.

At the same time the Modernist garden was rapidly developing in North America, spearheaded by Thomas Church, pioneer of the "California Style". Having studied at Harvard in the 1920s, Church created gardens following the four principles he outlined in his 1955 book, *Gardens are for People*: *unity, function, simplicity, and scale*. He argued that a garden should reflect its owners' lifestyle, functioning as an outdoor room where the family could extend their living, with free flow between the inside and outside. With his iconic design of the El Novillero ranch in 1947, consisting of a kidney-shaped pool, family areas, and architectural foliage, Church provided a blueprint for all future modern gardens.

The modern lifestyle

Meanwhile, England was emerging from postwar austerity in the early 1960s and looking to the future. Mid-century architecture followed the Californian style, with single-level homes and gardens that were treated as another living area, used for cooking, playing, and socializing. Aided by innovations such as home barbecues, patios, and sliding patio doors, the barrier between indoors and outdoors began to dissolve and the whole pattern of people's lifestyles changed.

Then, in 1962, driven by all these influences, John Brookes burst onto the stage at the Chelsea Flower Show with a revolutionary garden. A multifunctional outdoor room, this was a practical space as well as a design marvel, with a pergola for relaxing and entertaining, stylish seating, and modern sculpture, while the plants – rhododendrons, mahonia, and pyracantha – were used to provide structure, texture, and pops of colour. Lauded as the first garden at Chelsea to showcase garden design rather than just plants, it was a sensation.

In 1969, Brookes would clearly articulate his design manifesto – that gardens are fundamentally places for use by people, and an extension of the home – in his seminal book *Room Outside*. The new default for the modern English garden was now set. Brookes had instigated the shift away from the dominant Arts and Crafts style (see p.102) towards a contemporary concept that is still highly influential. Today, his designs are revamped with naturalistic planting and sustainable materials, but Brookes' guiding ethos of gardens being "for people" is unlikely to be replaced anytime soon.

John Brookes in 1962, studying the pergola in his award-winning Chelsea Flower Show exhibition garden

Denmans Garden

The home and workplace of landscape architect John Brookes for nearly 40 years, this glorious garden combines curves with geometric shapes to great effect.

Curving lawns, gravel paths, and sweeping borders of shrubs and herbaceous perennials in the outer garden at Denmans

Denmans Garden in West Sussex provides an insight into the mind of one of England's greatest Modernist landscape architects, John Brookes. It covers only 4 acres, but its clever progression of different shapes makes it feel larger.

Hugh and Joyce Robinson bought the property in 1946 and named it Denmans, after the family who once owned the surrounding estate. Joyce was a plantswoman extraordinaire: over time, she developed the garden, nurturing unusual plants in varying growing conditions. Inspired (like Sissinghurst's Vita Sackville-West) by a trip to the Greek island of Delos, Robinson used gravel to create her iconic dry river beds, predating Beth Chatto's experiments by some decades.

Impressed by Robinson's strong planting style, Brookes persuaded her to let him establish his teaching school – the Clock House School of Garden Design – at Denmans in 1980. Gradually, he took over the garden. He began by improving its flow, creating serpentine paths to accentuate the meandering borders and entice visitors to discover further planting areas. Mown differently each season to allow bulbs to recharge and grass to grow long, the paths terminate at a self-seeded beach area and natural pool.

Architectural approach

Denmans is a series of "outdoor rooms" within a Modernist grid of geometric shapes, linked by sweeping curves and architectural plants, such as *Euphorbia*, rather than formal hedges. Some spaces are expansive; others are intimate, such as the Walled Garden. Once a kitchen garden, this is now a rigidly geometric gravel garden, planted with tropical species including pomegranates.

The diversity of Brookes' planting – sometimes bold, at other times softened by what he called "pretties" – underlines his passion for foliage, flowers, and shapes, and gives Denmans a fascinating continuity of texture, colour, and structure. Brookes mocked his naturalistic approach as "self-seeded scattery", but it undoubtedly helped to set the trend for lower-maintenance gardens.

The herbaceous borders at Denmans brim with colour; here, the bright orange heleniums, dahlias, and red-hot pokers pop against the blue asters and aconites.

Landscape architect Geoffrey Jellicoe designed many iconic landscapes throughout his career, including the John F. Kennedy memorial in Runnymede, Surrey, but the private garden at Shute House in Dorset, designed in stages between 1969 and 1996, is arguably his finest work.

Birth and rebirth

In 1969, Michael and Anne Tree commissioned Jellicoe to create a garden at their home, Shute House. Jellicoe had previously worked for Michael's mother, Nancy Lancaster, at Ditchley Park in Oxfordshire. By this time, he was at the peak of his career, with a deep understanding of garden and landscape history, from the neoclassical through to the postmodern, and of the physical and subconscious elements of an English garden. Inspired by Swiss psychologist Carl Jung's work on the unconscious mind, Jellicoe was keen to test his theory that people react both consciously and subconsciously to their surroundings.

By the 1990s, the garden at Shute had fallen into decline, and the house's new owners, John and Suzy Lewis, approached Jellicoe in the hope that he would come out of retirement to restore and complete his masterpiece. It was to be his final project, but what he created was a work of genius – drawing on art, psychology, history, and philosophy, and using a limited palette of colours to create a contemporary experience much like that achieved by 18th-century landscape designer William Kent at Rousham in Oxfordshire (see p.52).

CASE STUDY

Shute House

A place of pilgrimage for garden historians, Geoffrey Jellicoe's final masterpiece cleverly combines water and woodland to create a serene space.

The formal rill, fed by the waters of the River Nadder, flows in through the centre of the garden, evoking a sense of orderly calm

above *The formal Canal Garden framed by beech, wisteria, and rhododendron;* **right** *Busts of Achilles, Neptune, and Zeus underline the classical influences at Shute*

All in the mind

For Jung, water often symbolized the unconscious, and consequently Jellicoe was fascinated by the use of water in landscape design. He deployed it to great effect in Shute's woodland setting, diverting the River Nadder to create the iconic bubble fountain, which feeds a formal narrow rill of flowing water. This in turn cascades over a succession of copper ledges, each producing a different musical note, before being reunited with a second channel – a mirror-like serpentine lake – in the Bog Garden. Water was key, according to Jellicoe: "There was never any doubt that it was the thought, presence, action, and sound of water that was holding together the competing ideas that had been introduced into the woodlands ..."

Twin grottos overlook the channels – another nod to William Kent. There is also a formal canal, a lily pool, and a stunning camellia walk. The garden concludes with a box amphitheatre, tucked behind a double bridge swathed in wisteria. From here, the visitor must return, meandering past sculptural elements, including an exedra (a type of seating area popular in ancient Greece and Rome) and a trio of classical busts positioned against a hedge, which underline the classical referencing of the English landscape garden and the gardens of Italy.

The overall effect is that of a sanctuary – a garden that demands contemplation. The black swans that float almost seamlessly along the naturalistic canal, in dramatic contrast to the mass of white arums planted along the bank, add to the otherworldliness of Shute. This is a place of such tranquillity and, indeed, creative stimulation, that it should, without question, be experienced at least once.

the

new

english

garden

Dutch New Naturalism

"I take a piece of natural landscape that I like and modify it to create a piece of garden."

Keith Wiley, Gardens Illustrated, *2019*

Planting design has changed radically in England over the last couple of decades, shifting towards a naturalistic style characterized by seemingly unstructured drifts of perennials and grasses, and this change has come largely from the Netherlands.

It is recognized that Dutch designer Piet Oudolf spearheaded the movement in 1999 when commissioned to revive the derelict walled garden at Scampston Hall in Malton. His design was a revelation: naturalistic and modern, yet surprisingly redolent of 17th-century English formality. Garden rooms were delineated by geometric hedges, with a pyramid-shaped mount, topiary, pleached lime trees, and a "Silent Garden" of yew pillars, all of which contrasts beautifully with the perennial meadow planting and swathes of undulating molinia grasses. It felt new, but Oudolf was in fact continuing a tradition that had begun long before. In the early 20th century in the Netherlands and Germany, perennials and grasses, largely from the abundant prairies of North America, were being propagated by master nurserymen such as Karl Foerster and sold throughout Europe, particularly to the Dutch Moerheim nursery, owned by Bonne Ruys. Ruys' daughter Mien (see p.150) – a natural genius – was soon experimenting with plant combinations and creating individual plots in which to display them; this became the Tuinen Mien Ruys, the garden she established in 1924, and so the revolution began.

"It all begins with Mien," Oudolf once said, which for the most part is true, but further acknowledgement must go to William Robinson (see p.104), who anticipated this quiet revolution in 1870 in his book *The Wild Garden*, with theories

that would be further disseminated by Gertrude Jekyll (see p.106). However, it was not until the late 20th century that the naturalistic planting ideal was truly formed, and although Oudolf was leading the invasion from the Netherlands, England had a few revolutionaries of its own.

The New Naturalism

From around the 1980s onwards, there were significant developments in what is now termed "New Naturalism" – planting in harmony with nature. Pam Lewis's incredible wildlife garden, Sticky Wicket, in Dorset, for example, was a haven of wildflowers and grasses, while at the Garden House, 10 acres on the edge of Dartmoor, Keith and Ros Wiley created one of the most innovative gardens in England between 1978 and 2003, with loose, almost wild planting in tune with the landscape – a concept they took to their next garden, Wildside.

As climate change became harder to ignore, many significant designers came on board with this idea of ecologically conscious gardening that encourages biodiversity, recognizing that naturalistic planting could contribute to the solution. Today it is seen as an obvious development, but change was slow in coming.

Again, it was a Dutch designer who would push the style forward. In 1999 Henk Gerritsen collaborated with keen conservationists Nicky and Strilli Oppenheimer to create a whole set of natural gardens at their organic, biodynamic farm, Waltham Place, in Berkshire. The result is informal to say the least, bordering on a wilderness in places, where even weeds can run free, and it remains one of England's outstanding gardens, though largely unknown.

In the last 20 years, the naturalistic movement has changed the English garden forever. It has inspired leading designers from Christopher Bradley-Hole and Brita von Schoenaich, to Dan Pearson, to James Hitchmough, and Nigel Dunnett, whose ground-breaking urban planting in Sheffield is nothing short of remarkable (see p.202). And, of course, it has spawned influential gardens all over the country, from the Sussex Prairie Garden – Britain's largest naturalistic offering – to Holbrook in Devon, where the ongoing experiments with planting and colour are overwhelming.

As such, it's an exciting time in garden design in England, and while Piet Oudolf rightly gets the lion's share of press coverage, it pays to remember that there is so much more going on.

Shimmering drifts of purple molinia grass in Piet Oudolf's contemporary walled garden at Scampston Hall

Hauser & Wirth Somerset

In this perfect pairing of gallery and garden, Piet Oudolf has used drifts
of colour and foliar texture to create an outdoor space for all seasons.

Oudolf Field, the perennial meadow created by Dutch star Piet Oudolf, leading to the Radić Pavilion

The Somerset town of Bruton is not an obvious location for an art gallery with outposts in Zurich, London, and New York, among others. But Hauser & Wirth Somerset, which opened in 2014, is a triumph. A restored farmstead – Durslade Farm – it houses exhibitions in its two gallery spaces, and the pasture beyond has been transformed by landscape designer Piet Oudolf, master of the naturalistic Dutch Wave planting technique.

Like the galleries, the garden is cleverly curated. It consists of three areas: the farmyard (a rectangular lawn edged with daisies), the cloister garden, and – the highlight – a 1.5-acre perennial meadow known as Oudolf Field. At first, we are offered mere glimpses of what lies ahead. The planting by the entrance is subtle, but unmistakably part of the Oudolf experience. In a courtyard between the galleries, the cloister garden has echoes of the English *hortus conclusus* ("enclosed garden"). Its restrained colour palette of grasses and perennials, planted beneath mulberry trees, forms a backdrop to the sculpture on display, and creates an area of calm before the main performance.

Perennial perfection

Moving back through the galleries, the full glory of Oudolf's planting is revealed, with its painterly swathes of textures and colours. Oudolf Field is made up of around 15 curved planting beds, which appear random but are, in fact, cleverly positioned on either side of a meandering gravel path. This, in turn, is broken up by circular grass beds. The beds are slightly elevated – a cunning way to tame the Somerset clay and ensure that the meadow plants can thrive in free-draining soil. Oudolf has employed his pioneering matrix planting style to great effect, interplanting a single perennial species, the grass *Sporobolus heterolepis*, with a select mix of complementary plants, including irises and *Dianthus* (pinks), to provide pops of colour.

right *View from the Radić Pavilion;* **far right**
The restrained Cloister Garden in shades of
green; **below** *Oudolf Field, with its loose drifts*
of colour and texture

Another classic Oudolf format – plant repetition – unifies the whole layout; *Veronicastrum virginicum* "Fascination" and *Liatris spicata* punctuate the beds. This style of planting means that the garden reaches its peak in autumn; however, in line with Oudolf's advocacy of seasonality and the need for a year-round backdrop to the galleries, the field is further planted with more than 25,000 spring bulbs.

The Radić Pavilion, designed by Chilean architect Smiljan Radić, looms over Oudolf Field like an extraterrestrial spaceship. This majestic structure provides a performance area, as well as a place to sit and admire the garden below.

A work of art

Hauser & Wirth and Piet Oudolf are a perfect match, with their thoughtful and sometimes provocative creative sensibilities intermingling in a synergy of colour and texture. Oudolf's masterful planting acknowledges the wider landscape without slavishly copying it, and as a result, the farm, galleries, and garden are at one with their surroundings. He has used traditional elements of surprise, yet these are cleverly contained within the garden's boundary. At no time does the energy of the planting spill out into the landscape beyond. The overall effect is artful – almost an installation in itself – and beautifully befits its setting.

Old styles return

> "We wanted something that was an offering up of nature to nature."

Tom Stuart-Smith, The English Garden Magazine, *2017*

It might seem as though there is really only one garden style these days, that of Dutch-inspired naturalism. The truth is, however, that there are now a multitude of different trends forming, which see old styles of the past reinterpreted with a modern twist.

A new formality

Primarily, there has been a strong return to formality, though in a looser format than the 17th-century version. Several designers champion the style, but few match the output of Arne Maynard, who has helped refresh many outstanding historic gardens, among them the vast Gordon Castle Walled Garden in Moray, and Renishaw Hall, home of the Sitwell family.

Like many others, Maynard has returned to topiary, that fundamental formal element, to add quirky structure to his garden schemes. At Haddon Hall in Derbyshire, one of England's earliest Renaissance gardens, Maynard's job was to recapture its historical, romantic spirit. The result is a joyful interplay between formality and informality, with asymmetrical topiary offset by blousy roses and naturalistic planting, such as the wildflower meadows that blend into the fields beyond.

Formal features evidently remain an enduring fascination: the extraordinary topiary shapes at Cressy Hall in Lincolnshire range from pyramids to tiered obelisks to the indefinable; at Broughton Grange in Oxfordshire Tom Stuart-Smith has entirely reimagined traditional parterres, rose gardens, and knot gardens (see p.200), while East Ruston Old Vicarage near Norwich (see p.170) always leaves me speechless with its eclectic take on modern formality.

The perennial cottage garden

The cottage garden is always present in garden design, though today's version has little to do with Gertrude Jekyll (see p.106) and more to do with environmental action, prioritizing colour, scent and pollen-rich plants to draw in wildlife. Few gardens are a better advert for the style than Sarah Raven's Perch Hill Farm, East Sussex, an organic cutting garden, which is a masterclass in floriferous abundance and bold colour combinations. An author and businesswoman, Raven is connected to Sissinghurst (see p.118) through marriage, and she continues Vita Sackville-West's glorious tradition of plantsmanship, continually trialling and experimenting with plants to sell through her business.

Classic revival

In another revision of an old style, many traditional country house gardens are being given a refresh, which includes abundant modern planting that is environmentally conscious, while retaining strong elements of the beloved Arts and Crafts garden that has expressed "Englishness" since the Victorian era.

The stunning Armscote Manor, near Stratford-upon-Avon, designed by Dan Pearson, is a classic example – a series of enclosed garden rooms with bold, naturalistic planting mixed with hard landscaping and sweeping views. Some, like the highly conceptual Plaz Metaxu in Devon (see p.175), would not look out of place during the English Landscape Movement, resplendent with classical iconography yet with a modern slant; others are full of surprises, like Parsonage Farm in Kirdford, East Sussex, a unique garden, which is formal in parts and naturalistic in others, filled with outstanding contemporary sculpture – enjoy the giraffes!

With such remarkable variety, plantsmanship, and design skill currently being employed, the English garden is in very safe hands. There may not be one decisive style at play, but the excitement these gardens create feeds the imagination and promises a bright future.

The intricate topiary shapes at Cressy Hall in Lincolnshire, created by owner and amateur gardener Michael Hill, breathe new life into an ancient art

East Ruston Old Vicarage

Although this garden is now structurally complete, its creators have vowed to continue to develop new planting, making it one of the most exciting "new" gardens in England.

Lying close to the north Norfolk coast, and at odds with the farmland that surrounds it, the garden at East Ruston Old Vicarage is a jewel in the crown of English gardens. It was created over the span of more than 40 years by its owners, amateur-turned-professional horticulturalists Alan Gray and Graham Robeson.

The site's innovative planting, contained within a surprisingly traditional formal design, reflects the flamboyance and compatibility of its makers (who, in this regard, could be likened to Sissinghurst's creators, Vita Sackville-West and Harold Nicolson). Indeed, the comparison with Sissinghurst (see p.118) is not lost as you move around the garden's differing areas, or "rooms", with their ingenious use of hedges and trees that alternately restrict and reveal the view.

Gray and Robeson bought the house, along with 2 acres of uncultivated land, in 1973. Bit by bit, they have developed and extended the bleak and unpromising plot to create a remarkable 32-acre garden that includes fine herbaceous borders, gravel gardens, a large woodland garden, and a desert garden, to name a few. The couple are justifiably proud of their achievements, and the coat of arms they have installed above the so-called "Postman's Gate" entrance to the garden includes the motto *Concilio et Labore*, meaning "by council and labour" – a humorous nod to the way in which the garden was developed.

Exploring the garden

The King's Walk stretches out from the back of the house and is the central focus of the garden. It is unashamedly formal, consisting of three separate, immaculately mown lawns, each subtly higher than the previous one, enclosed within high hedges.

above *Winding through the Woodland Garden;* **top** *The tiered King's Walk, leading to the pavilion;* **right** *Sun-loving plants in the walled Mediterranean Garden*

Ten tall, tightly clipped yew cones lead the visitor onwards to a brick gateway topped with terracotta balls, and then beyond to the pyramidal pavilion, where the King's Walk ends and the dry Mediterranean Garden, enclosed within warming brick walls, begins.

More traditional still is the sunken rose garden, lowered to provide shelter from the North Sea winds. This tranquil space contrasts with the abundance of its neighbour, the Exotic Garden. Here, *Musa basjoo* (Japanese banana), palm trees, impatiens (busy lizzies), cannas, salvias, and the brightest of dahlias dazzle, surrounded by lush foliage. But the central fountain, designed by Giles Raynor, steals the show, with its inward-flowing water that prevents visitors from being soaked by unruly spray.

The gardens continue through the Orangery Border and Green Court, then along the Apple Walk, which concludes with a magnificent view of the church on the coast at Happisburgh. Other highlights include the Dutch Garden, a box parterre that is planted for colour in spring and summer, as well as the gloriously romantic Glasshouse Garden, the Winter Garden (which offers a glimpse of Happisburgh Lighthouse), and, lastly, the Diamond Jubilee Walled Garden – Gray and Robeson's tribute to Queen Elizabeth II and their final massive architectural project (built in 2012).

left *The fountain and wildlife ponds in the Exotic Garden;* **top left** *The Exotic Garden;* **above** Rosa *'Maigold' adorns the arches in the Glasshouse Garden*

Eccentricity

"Surprise is one of the chief delights of a garden."

George Carter, The Independent, *1995*

There are always gardens that stand out as both exceptional and noticeably different to the prevailing style. They might be called "eccentric", but really, these gardens simply have a design aesthetic that is particular to their creators – sometimes obsessive, sometimes unusual, but always full of wonder.

Earthforms

Few landscape architects are as distinctive as Kim Wilkie, who has for over 25 years been creating "earthforms" that look more like art installations than gardens. Very much in the 18th-century tradition of complementing rather than imposing on the landscape, but with a contemporary edge, Wilkie's designs have a sympathetic yet remarkable impact.

At Boughton House, Northamptonshire, for example, he created *Orpheus* as part of the Duke of Buccleugh's innovative restoration of the formal gardens. Inspired by the sheer scale of the park, Wilkie matched the towering Olympian Mount with a 7-m-(23-ft-) deep inverted grass pyramid that you can descend, like Orpheus

into the underworld, via the angular terraced path to the reflective pool at the base.

This use of grassed terracing is a favourite feature of Wilkie's. At Great Fosters, Surrey, the garden terminates in a tiered, turfed amphitheatre, while at Heveningham Hall, Suffolk, a magical Fibonacci fan of ascending terraces encompasses the mature trees. These sculptural forms sit in unexpected harmony with the landscape, and are unmistakably Wilkie's work.

Garden of surprises

Working on similar precepts, George Carter is a garden maker in the London and Wise tradition (see p.24), Baroque and proud, yet who wittily modernizes formal principles and utterly rejects "garden fashions". His striking use of parterres, geometric pattern, and topiary can be seen at various majestic gardens, including Thenford (see p.186) and Somerleyton Hall in Suffolk, but Carter reaches his most playful at the Garden of Surprises at Burghley House, Lincolnshire. This Elizabethan-inspired garden is all about

entertainment, replete with swivelling Caesar busts, a moss house, a mirror maze, and numerous *giochi d'acqua* (water jokes), with jets springing up from hidden fountains and trickling down rills into a shell grotto. Tucked away within a grand rigid structure of obelisks, gold finials, and trelliswork, it's a unique – and yes, surprising – take on the formal garden.

The conceptual garden

Then there is the outstanding high-concept garden Plaz Metaxu (Greek for "the place between"), which was begun in 1992 in a Devon valley by art historian Alasdair Forbes. Influenced by Greek mythology, sublime poetry, and post-Jungian psychology, Plaz Metaxu is a modern reinterpretation of the English landscape garden, and it takes you on a revelatory journey.

A mix of carefully planted courtyards, walled gardens, open landscape, lake, and woodland, the garden is arranged into areas, each dedicated to a Classical deity, with inscriptions, standing stones, and artfully placed urns acting as both sculpture and poetic references. Designed to serve every emotion, this is a hugely significant garden full of subtlety and abstract ideas, which should be experienced at least once in every garden visitor's life.

With so many oddities, quirks, and surprises to be seen across the country, we needn't worry that the English garden is at all predictable. If these gloriously idiosyncratic gardens are anything to go by, English eccentricity is going strong.

Orpheus by Kim Wilkie at Boughton House, Northamptonshire; created in 2007–2009, this strikingly modern "earthform" within the vast 18th-century parkland represents a journey into Hades

Of course, it's not just the men who have been busy expressing their individuality through garden design. In recent decades, numerous plantswomen have come to the fore who, like the great Beth Chatto, are doing things their own way, creating gardens that are experimental, fascinating, influential, and often wondrously indefinable.

Old and new

The garden at Westwell Manor, in Oxfordshire, created by the late gardening genius Anthea Gibson between 1979 and 2010, is one of those that stands out. Made up of 12 garden rooms, the 7-acre site is in many ways traditional, with a knot garden, potager, herbaceous borders, and topiary, but it also has some startlingly modern elements that make it worthy of pages of description.

The reflective black pool is addictive; it merges seamlessly with the surrounding grass and usually has a boat floating upon it, wittily tied to a Venetian pole. This wit is repeated throughout, with topiary birds and a group of pleached trees centrally planted in a lawned area. Indeed, lawns are a masterful feature at Westwell, either dissected diagonally by slim borders of lavender, carved into an earthwork to reflect a nearby outbuilding, or laid in a rigid strip with rills and avenues of pleached lime trees running along each side. Then we encounter the Moonlight Garden, a circle of yew hedges that contains a stunning selection of white and silver foliage plants that glimmer at night. As a whole, Westwell is a masterpiece that ignores garden fashions and is packed full of experimental ideas.

The mathematical garden

Then, in nearby Gloucestershire, we have Througham Court, originally created in the 1930s by Arts and Crafts architect Norman Jewson but developed since 2000 by Dr Christine Facer Hoffman – an award-winning scientist and landscape architect – into one of the most unique gardens in England. A "laboratory" of sorts, the garden reflects Facer Hoffman's obsession with scientific theories, mathematical formulae, and numerical patterns that occur in nature. With names such as the Cosmic Evolution Garden (where stone globes representing planets are inscribed with the six numbers said to underpin the origins of the universe) and Fibonacci's Walk (a path where birch trees are planted at distances that follow the number sequence), you know each area, or "fragment", will be a visual treat.

Of course, there is beautiful planting everywhere, but it's the many thought-provoking installations that elevate this garden, including a seat that represents a black hole, which is deliberately difficult to get out of, and the Chiral Terrace, with its asymmetrical chequerboard floor representing forms that cannot be superimposed on their mirror image. Througham Court is an experience, where art, science, and nature meet; expect your senses to be stimulated and your mind stretched (and sometimes confounded) as you follow its fascinating narrative.

A topiary wonderland

Finally, few others can rival Charlotte Molesworth's garden in Benenden, Kent, for boundless English character and charm. Based almost entirely around topiary – clipped into every shape and form imaginable – the garden is an eccentric delight, rather like a children's fairy tale. Molesworth, who was once an art teacher, has such an energy and enthusiasm for the craft of topiary that it feels infectious, and her skills are much in demand for obvious reasons.

Once the kitchen garden of plant collector Collingwood "Cherry" Ingram, the garden has taken over 40 years to develop and is a remarkable confection of peacocks, spirals, chess pieces, rabbits, and possibly even a dog or two. Surrounding the picture-perfect Balmoral Cottage, it has evolved with an almost timeless elegance, capturing a magical sense of "old England"; it's a garden where you could easily get lost and definitely host a mad hatter's tea party!

It's exhilarating and gratifying to find women – excluded from the horticultural establishment for so long – at the very heart of progressive garden design today. Freed from convention, they are producing some of the most thrilling, adventurous, and pioneering gardens in England.

BETH CHATTO
1923–2018

Beth Chatto was a champion of ecological gardening and a pioneer of the "right plant, right place" approach. She began her world-renowned garden at Elmstead Market in Essex after being encouraged and advised by her close friend and horticultural hero Sir Cedric Morris (see p.122). Fundamental to Beth's gardening ethos was the work of her husband, Andrew Chatto. His research into plant ecology enabled him to exhaustively catalogue plants by their geographical location, charting the climate, conditions, and vegetation of each area, as well as the prominent plant communities and ancestors of garden plants found there. When Beth had a new plant, she could discover its original habitat and the conditions it needed to thrive – and so the revolutionary ethos of "right plant, right place" was born.

Drifts of alstroemerias, poppies, and euphorbias swirl around conifers and yuccas in the drought-resistant planting of the Gravel Garden, Beth Chatto Gardens, Essex.

Highgrove

A modern ethos of sustainability and conservation lies at the heart of this very traditional royal garden.

The Thyme Walk, where thyme, marjoram, and primroses replace grass, while the eccentric yew topiary leads to the house

Highgrove, the private home of King Charles III and Camilla, Queen Consort, is said to define the ecological principles the King, as Prince of Wales, has championed for decades – and, indeed, it proves that the highest aesthetic standards can be achieved using organic methods. But it is a troubling garden on many levels, not least because the necessary security prevents visitors from taking photographs, using mobile phones, or wandering the grounds unattended.

The King bought the estate, near Tetbury in Gloucestershire, in 1980, and proceeded to overhaul the garden, helped by two horticultural legends: Miriam Rothschild and Rosemary Verey. Rothschild, with her pioneering emphasis on preserving wild meadows and protecting native species, was clearly an inspiration to the then Prince Charles; meanwhile, the touch of Verey, the doyenne of the country house set, is evident in Highgrove's traditional planting.

Formal fashion

The initial appearance of the 15-acre garden is one of controlled formality. From the house, which was built in the 1790s, the central feature is the Thyme Walk, with its whimsical golden yew topiary. True to tradition, this ends beyond the Lily Pool Garden with an eye-catcher: the bronze Borghese Gladiator. The eye is then drawn to the Dovecote, via the Lime Avenue. There is nothing radical here, and yet it is lovely nonetheless.

At the statue we turn right on our guided tour to view the Laurel Tunnel and Buttress Garden, with its rhododendrons. Nearing the house, the influence of Verey is evident in the romantic Rose Pergola and quintessentially English Cottage Garden. Totally different in style is the exotic Carpet Garden.

This stunning re-creation of a Persian garden, based on the King's sketch of a Turkish carpet, won an award at the 2001 RHS Chelsea Flower Show.

Another Highgrove highlight is the Wildflower Meadow. Created by Rothschild, this haven for native flora and fauna is magnificent in the early summer sunshine. Moving on, the fern-filled Stumpery designed by contemporary duo Julian and Isabel Bannerman exudes Victorian splendour, and among its intricately carved classical temples, the amusingly titled Temple of Worthies references a similarly named structure at Stowe (see p.62). Nearby, the thatched treehouse where princes William and Harry once played still stands.

The formal Kitchen Garden would rival any county show vegetable display, with its exquisitely neat rows of produce. From here, we progress to the Arboretum. Nestled among the trees is the architecturally unconventional Sanctuary, a private space for the King to retreat to. This offers a stunningly contained view of the Sundial Garden and the house beyond.

A principled place

Highgrove is an intriguing garden. While the methods used to manage it in an organic, sustainable way are undeniably innovative, the planting and layout cannot be said to be revolutionary. But away from the strictly controlled tour, certain higgledy-piggledy details detract from the garden's formality – after all, the King has to find a place for all the gifts he receives, however bizarre! If you can ignore the wooden mushrooms and confusing mass of tree ferns, Highgrove is a beautiful, though very traditional, garden that practises what it preaches.

left Gunnera manicata *sits on a stone tower at the heart of the Stumpery;* **below** *The Wildflower Meadow, planted with camassias and alliums*

Country estates revisited

"The most magical moment in gardens is on the cusp of chaos."

Jane Hurst, House & Garden, *2022*

Despite the move over the centuries towards smaller-scale garden making, there are still vast country-estate gardens being created throughout England. In the post-colonial era, many estates proved too expensive for hereditary families to maintain; they were either taken over by heritage organizations, repurposed, or, in some cases, left to fall into dereliction.

By necessity, then, many of England's privately owned estates have had to evolve into something much more innovative than simply a private pleasure palace for the elite; owners have had to revamp and rethink to create multipurpose visitor attractions that can sustain themselves. Obviously, these projects are all subject to massive investment by the owners, but the best examples are making a significant contribution to garden making today.

Restoration

One poignant example is St Giles House in Dorset, which was uninhabited for decades after the Second World War. When it was inherited under tragic circumstances in 2005 by Nicholas Ashley-Cooper, the 12th Earl of Shaftesbury, the dilapidated 17th-century house and garden must have seemed overwhelming. In 2010, however, he began a major award-winning restoration project, aided in 2013 by garden designer Jane Hurst.

The goal was not to create a slavish reconstruction of the garden's past, but a modern garden for the 21st century. So while the serpentine lake, statues, and 18th-century follies have been restored, the new scheme is romantic and dramatic, but also easy to maintain, sustainable, and wildlife-friendly, with bold, colourful perennial planting inspired by Gertrude

Jekyll around the house and formations of copper beech trees punctuating the landscape – an outstanding example of an estate brought back from the brink.

Reinvention

Other estates are finding a whole new purpose. Nevill Holt in Leicestershire, for example, has been reimagined as a cultural venue since David Ross bought it in 2000. It now hosts Nevill Holt Opera, while the gardens, designed by Rupert Golby, provide a glorious setting for modern art, with sculptures by Antony Gormley and Allen Jones, which complement the architectural planting.

Perhaps the most exciting reinvention, however, is that of Hadspen House, former estate of the Hobhouse family, in Somerset. Made famous by horticultural icon Penelope Hobhouse, and inspirational gardeners Nori and Sandra Pope, who experimented with ground-breaking colour schemes there from the 1980s, the garden is now a crucial part of the estate's new incarnation: luxury hotel, the Newt. The garden was designed by Patrice Taravella for South African owners Karen Roos and Koos Bekker to be both ornamental and useful, and it more than meets the brief. Centred around the walled Parabola – a beautifully formal nod to the Baroque, which contains an apple-tree maze – is a hothouse redolent of obsessive Victorian plant collectors; a produce garden, providing for the hotel and restaurants; a treetop walkway; a cider distillery; an apiary; even a re-created Roman villa. The modern, naturalistic planting, with nods to the Popes' renowned colour schemes, holds it all together.

The Newt is Disneyland for horticulturalists. To call it just a garden is an injustice; it is more a destination, and a remarkable example of how country estates do not have to live in the past.

The working country estate at the Newt in Somerset, where traditional grounds have been reimagined to stunning, modern effect

Thenford

In the great tradition of English landscape gardening, the creation of a fine and extensive garden is the ultimate legacy for a politician of status. Thenford in Northamptonshire is the modern equivalent, and the politician is Michael Heseltine, along with his wife, Anne.

Described by architectural historian Nikolaus Pevsner as "decidedly conservative for its date", Thenford House was built in the 18th century in the Palladian style. It is surrounded by 70 acres of grand formal gardens, with woodland planting and a large lake. But this traditional formula does not detract from Thenford's charm.

Over more than 40 years, with the help of leading horticulturalists of their time, including Lanning Roper, Harold Hillier, Roy Lancaster, and Keith Rushforth, the Heseltines have lovingly restored the derelict estate, and have created one of the finest landscape gardens of modern times.

Modern formality

The Arboretum, which is the main focus of the landscape, features a collection of more than 3,000 different trees and shrubs and exudes 18th-century grandeur.

But it is the Formal Gardens that have allowed the Heseltines to reveal their personalities, and this indulgence makes them Thenford's greatest asset. Designed by George Carter, the walled garden is magnificent. It follows the classic formal division into quarters, but Carter has expressed his genius with the use of copper-domed pavilions, wooden obelisks, an aviary, mirror pools, fruit cages, a cottage *ornée* (a stylized rustic building), and, at the centre, a Coanda water sculpture by William Pye.

The contemporary Rill Garden pays tribute to the great garden makers of Italy, and according to Anne was inspired by visits to the famous gardens of Villa Lante in Italy. (It is also reminiscent of Geoffrey Jellicoe's gardens at Shute House, see p.156.) A channel of water – the rill – runs down a beautifully formal hillside, ending up in designer

above *A sculptural beech hedge in the Walled Garden;* **top** *The Arboretum, with willow and Japanese maple in autumnal colour;* **right** *The obelisks and pavilions of the Formal Gardens*

left *The Rill Garden;* **centre** *Sculpture by Elisabeth Frink, one of many artworks in the Sculpture Garden;* **right** *Gated entrance to the Trough Garden*

Maggy Howarth's glorious pool, which is shaped like a scallop shell and decorated with a delicate pattern of coloured pebbles and seashells.

A sense of humour

Anne Heseltine designed and curated the Sculpture Garden, which has a "modern British" theme. Each sculpture is enclosed within a series of rooms, defined by beech and yew hedging and designed to be magnificent all year round. The greatest of modern British sculptors are represented here, with works by Elisabeth Frink, Lynn Chadwick, Laura Ford, and Ronald Rae. But it is the monumental bronze sculpture of Lenin, taken from the roof of the KGB headquarters in Preili, Latvia, after the fall of communism, that brings the greatest surprise and delight. The Russian revolutionary casting an approving eye over a garden created by a Conservative grandee hints at a glorious sense of humour.

Playful touches are also evident in the Trough Garden. Stone troughs are filled with tiny alpines, taking the planting to a micro level, yet the garden is entered by the grandest of gates, suggesting a whole different planting experience. With this and other delightful optical illusions, Thenford reveals a great personality in its creators – one indicative of so many renowned garden makers (but not, it has to be said, of many politicians).

Garden sanctuaries

"It just makes me so happy ... if nature was on prescription for mental health, we'd all be better off."

Butter Wakefield, Evening Standard, *2017*

Over the past few years, as we've faced a global pandemic and the isolation that came with it, gardens have become a sanctuary for many, particularly in harsh urban environments where having a place to relax, clear our thoughts, and be in harmony with nature is a true luxury. In consequence, urban gardens are having a moment, with design styles ranging from urban courtyard, to urban meadow, to minimal, to contemporary. Enticing us from the glossy pages of magazines and aspirational TV shows, the urban garden – as a refuge, as an entertainment space, and as a design statement – is here to stay.

Inner-city oases

It doesn't get any more urban than London's East End, and while Spitalfields might seem an unlikely area for horticultural creativity, deep in Fournier Street and neighbouring Wilkes Street, hidden behind fine 17th-century French Huguenot weavers' houses, are a succession of small courtyard gardens that are havens of tranquillity. Each has its own microclimate, enabling lush growth, particularly of exotic plants, and some of them can be visited when they open for the National Garden Scheme. They always attract a large group of enthusiasts.

Further west, in Stamford Brook, garden designer Butter Wakefield has created a flower-filled country garden behind her Victorian townhouse, packed with foxgloves, geums, roses, and geraniums. She has masterfully developed a wildflower meadow bursting with wild daisies and knapweed towards the rear, while abundant perennial borders, which have been beautifully curated in flourishes of blues and pinks, are contained by clipped box pyramids. The whole composition is a textbook lesson in creating an oasis of calm and exemplifies the urban meadow style – you would truly think you were in the Cotswolds.

Modern masterpieces

Working from a minimalist perspective, Tom Stuart-Smith has deconstructed the urban garden simply but beautifully in a courtyard in Islington, north London. The space is dominated by tree ferns, underplanted by Japanese forest grass and box balls, and ascends via a stone stairway to a patio of block paving, leading towards a concealed children's sandpit. With its restricted green colour palette and otherworldly shapes, offset by the glass exterior of the newly refurbished house and concrete terrace, all is texture and shadow and light – part tropical forest, part alien landscape.

Gavin McWilliam and Andrew Wilson, the darlings of the RHS Show Garden scene, have worked on every kind of site, from urban rooftops to country estates, but it is in urban and suburban gardens that they excel. In Wimbledon, for example, they have created a stunning modern garden that redefines the suburban retreat. The naturalistic planting is framed within graphic trimmed hedges and sleek hard landscaping dotted with black stone containers crammed with plants. The effect is so successful that the pair have replicated it in many other gardens.

Urban gardens have truly benefited from the expansion of beautifully crafted landscaped design coupled with rich natural planting. The masters are showing us that there is no reason anymore to settle for a square lawn with thin borders around the edges, when we could have a bold,

above *A path winds through the soft grasses and wildflowers in Butter Wakefield's urban meadow garden at Stamford Brook;* **left** *Huge tree ferns create a stark look at this Islington courtyard garden by Tom Stuart-Smith*

> **" I try to work with clients who have the same values as me, who are interested in the environment and in the process of making a garden rather than having it as a showpiece. "**
>
> *Cleve West,* Gardens Illustrated, *2009*

imaginative, restorative sanctuary on our doorstep instead.

Natural care

The health benefits of gardens and gardening, for both mind and body, have always been well known. However, over the last 25 years or so, the theory has been put into practice by the introduction of beautiful gardens at medical centres to help support patients and their families while undergoing treatment. Hugely successful, the initiative has grown into a network of magical therapeutic spaces across the country where patients can find refuge in nature.

Maggie's centres

The first to establish the practice was cancer-support charity Maggie's, founded by Maggie Keswick and her husband Charles Jencks. Maggie's experience while being treated for breast cancer soon had the couple discussing the need for a more nurturing, comforting environment where patients and families could share time together and live well during treatment. The couple believed

design could play a significant role in healing, calling it the "Architecture of Hope", and so Maggie's centres are always unique, often award-winning buildings designed by leading architects, with beautifully thought-out gardens created by outstanding landscape designers.

The first Maggie's centre opened in 1996; today there are 29, reaching across the UK and as far as Tokyo. Each centre aims to achieve a strong connection with its surroundings, which informs its ethos. Maggie's West London, for example, with its uplifting orange exterior and flexible open spaces that transition into the garden, designed by Dan Pearson, seamlessly integrates indoor and outdoor. The protective birch trees, snug courtyards planted with architectural exotics, and meandering approach cocoon visitors in a pocket of calm within the hectic city.

Horatio's Garden

Another charity, Horatio's Garden – named after Horatio Chapple, a teenage volunteer at the Duke of Cornwall Spinal Treatment Centre in Salisbury who was tragically killed by a polar bear attack on a

trip in 2011 – has a similar remit. It was Horatio's idea to create gardens allied to NHS spinal-injury units, designed to offer patients and families a quiet, accessible, beautiful place to relax and connect. Created by top horticulturalists, the gardens are intended as the ultimate healing spaces, designed to reduce outside noise, with planting that stimulates the senses and encourages wildlife. For each one the charity funds a head gardener to ensure quality maintenance and provide gardening workshops.

To date, the charity has funded six UK gardens out of an intended 10. The first, completed in 2012 at the hospital Horatio volunteered at, was created by multi-award-winning designer Cleve West and set the standard, with clever, spine-shaped limestone seating, a long rill burbling with water, textural grasses, scented herbs, and colourful perennials. The latest, by Andy Sturgeon, will be at Musgrave Park Hospital, Belfast, and looks to be the best yet.

These stunning architectural projects are strong advocates for the healing power of gardens, offering physical relaxation, sensory stimulation and, as psychotherapist Sue Stuart-Smith writes in *The Well Gardened Mind*, "quiet, so you can hear your own thoughts". As such, they meet a fundamental human need, providing sanctuary from difficult treatments that can involve months in hospital with little or no access to nature. This truly inspired development should be expanded until all patients have access to such gardens.

Horatio's Garden South West, by Cleve West, at the Salisbury District Hospital, combines 23 trees, including Amelanchier lamarckii, *with sensory grasses, herbs, and perennials*

Prospect Cottage

A true work of art, Derek Jarman's extraordinary coastal garden at Dungeness was created as a project of defiance, healing, and hope.

Dungeness, the southernmost tip of Kent and home to a nuclear power station, is an extraordinary place to build a garden. But this barren landscape became a sanctuary for film director and artist Derek Jarman, who bought Prospect Cottage, a Victorian fisherman's hut, in 1987 after being diagnosed with HIV. For Jarman, gardening was an act of love, grief, and healing, and, as he wrote in his journals (collated in *Modern Nature*, 1992), his garden was "a memorial, each circular bed and dial a true lover's knot".

Weatherproofed with tar in the traditional way, the timber walls of Prospect Cottage are black and defiant against the elements, with one wall decorated with lines from John Donne's poem "The Sun Rising". The hut stands on a shingle beach, and it is here that Jarman began creating a garden, digging manure from a local farm into small holes in the shingle and using hardy plants, such as lavender, that could survive the coastal weather. Describing his first months there, Jarman wrote that "people thought I was building a garden for magical purposes – a white witch out to get the nuclear power station".

Creating a paradise

The garden at the front of the house began as a series of formal geometric shapes defined by foraged white flint. Over time, Jarman embellished these with other stones and flotsam, and planted salvias and poppies. To the side of the hut, the formal layout merges into the cottage garden, a loose arrangement of flotsam gathered from the nearby beach, dotted with tough, salt-loving, endemic beach plants. The sharp architectural form and vibrant colour of these plants and the roughness of the flotsam stand out against the sea-smoothed shingle, which appears to go on

left *John Donne's 1633 poem "The Sun Rising"
on the cottage exterior;* **top** *The coastal garden
and shingle beach;* **above** *Jarman's hardy seaside
planting set against the power station beyond*

left *Pebble sculpture with California poppies;*
centre *Driftwood sculpture with sea kale beyond;*
right *Metal sculpture made with flotsam*

and on. Jarman relished the lack of definition to the garden's borders, writing: "But above all I love that, visually, the garden doesn't end" (*Derek Jarman's Garden*, 1995).

One story tells of the horticultural luminaries Beth Chatto and Christopher Lloyd coming across Prospect Cottage and its garden in 1990, attracted by the brilliant colours of its flowers. Jarman was at home and, recognizing the pair, came out to greet them. Chatto later acknowledged that Prospect Cottage was the inspiration for the Gravel Garden at her famous garden in Essex (see p.178).

Jarman regarded his garden (a "paradise") as the antithesis of postmodern gardens, decrying their sterility, lack of personality, and disregard for their situation or place. On his death in 1994 from an AIDS-related illness, he left behind not only a huge artistic legacy, in the shape of his films, books, and paintings, but also a powerful horticultural one: a garden shaped by grief and hope in the face of an incurable illness. When Jarman's partner, Keith Collins, died in 2018, the fate of the house and garden seemed uncertain, but a fundraising drive led by the charity Art Fund has since raised more than £3 million, which has secured Prospect Cottage's future as one of the most visited and influential gardens in the country.

New
stars

"If everyone takes small steps
it can lead to big change."

Tom Massey, House & Garden, *2021*

Garden making is in a fantastic place right now; many new sites are being created that have the potential to engage young gardeners, bring new designers to the fore, and inspire all of us with fresh ideas.

Taking responsibility

Harris Bugg Studio, formed in 2017 by Charlotte Harris and Hugo Bugg, has risen fast after successive achievements, including three gold medals at Chelsea. Their progressive ethos is driven by the principle of "the common good", based on respecting people, place, and planet in every project. Their designs are recognized for telling stories about the site to reflect its spirit, and this approach is perfectly exemplified in their beautiful Kitchen Garden at the new RHS Garden Bridgewater in Salford, opened in 2021.

Within the Victorian walls, they took inspiration for the intricate layout of over 100 planting beds from the area's rich industrial heritage, in particular the original routes of the Bridgewater Canal and local field boundaries. The site's history is further referenced by water tanks and towers for climbing plants to romp through. Intended to motivate gardeners to grow their own, this experimental productive garden adopts a permaculture approach of reproducing natural ecosystems. The result is triumphant, mixing beauty, storytelling and ecological purpose.

Likewise, Tom Massey, one of today's most influential new thinkers in garden making, advocates working with, rather than against, nature to create sustainable, ecological, and beautiful modern gardens that support local wildlife and biodiversity. His approach is perfectly exemplified in the ground-breaking Yeo Valley Organic Garden he created for Chelsea in 2021 – its first organic show garden, and the first to be approved by the Soil Association. Combining Massey's designer's eye with climate awareness, the Yeo Valley garden

unsurprisingly won both a gold medal and the BBC People's Choice Award.

Taking risks

It takes a leap of faith to create a garden, but you don't need to be a trained horticulturalist to succeed. The self-taught Kenneth Roscoe transferred his skills in architectural design to his garden at Stretton Old Hall in Cheshire, reinterpreting a formal theme into something incredibly new that excels in every way. Head gardener Stephen Gore has referred to the style as "controlled exuberance", and you can see why. The garden is structured into a series of interconnected garden rooms, tightly curated and rigid, but the planting is magnificently abundant; all colour and texture, with features that play with shape

and scale. (I covet the gnarled old olive trees in vast terracotta pots that line the central pathway.) Water and modern sculpture bring continuity, while in every direction you are presented with visionary design ideas, before the garden slowly progresses towards a lake and open wildflower meadows. The garden is just a few years old but is so confident, so complete, it looks like it could have been there much longer. Bewilderingly brilliant in its plantsmanship and design, it is surely one of the finest gardens in England today.

Such newcomers as these encapsulate all that is great about modern garden making – contemporary in design, climate aware, big on ideas, and full of inspiration, with plants of all types grown to magnificent quality. Gardening legacies are being created as we speak.

Tom Massey and Sarah Mead's Yeo Valley Organic Garden at the RHS Chelsea Flower Show in 2021; all of the plants were organically grown in Somerset

Broughton Grange

One of Tom Stuart-Smith's greatest designs, this innovative garden blends old and new to masterful effect.

Broughton Grange, near Banbury in Oxfordshire, has a remarkable horticultural heritage, counting many of the Bloomsbury Group of artists and intellectuals, including Sissinghurst's Vita Sackville-West, among its visitors. By the time Stephen and Suzy Hester bought the property in 1992, however, it was desperately in need of renovation. With the help of landscape designer Tom Stuart-Smith, the Hesters have turned Broughton Grange into one of the most beautiful contemporary gardens in England.

Trio of terraces

Stuart-Smith transformed a south-facing slope, with stunning views over the Oxfordshire countryside, into a three-tiered set of terraces: the Walled Garden. The top terrace has prairie planting – a masterful mix of perennials and drifts of grasses, boldly punctuated with fastigiate yews. At the centre of the middle terrace is a reflective pond, crossed with stepping stones that appear to float and connected to the upper terrace by a sharply modern rill. The dreamy shapes of tall perennials contrast with the formally clipped beech topiary. Stuart-Smith's iconic parterre garden occupies the lower terrace. Its ground-breaking planting imitates the microscopic shapes created by the leaf cell structures of oak, beech, and ash trees.

By contrast, the romantic Knot Garden, edged in York stone, and the Parterre and Rose Garden are surprisingly traditional. An orchard, conventional herbaceous borders, and a sunken garden are lent an air of maturity by the majestic trees that remain. Many new trees have also been planted, and the 80-acre Arboretum will only improve with age.

Stuart-Smith teamed up with architect Ptolemy Dean to create the garden's hard landscaping, including the three stepped walls of the Walled Garden, as well as gates, entrances, and buildings. The success of their partnership echoes that of Nathaniel Lloyd and Edwin Lutyens at Great Dixter (see p.110) – and Broughton Grange, too, belongs with it in the illustrious ranks of great gardens.

The natural city

"People really respond to colourful naturalistic planting."

Nigel Dunnett, Gardens Illustrated, *2022*

There has been a remarkable change in urban planning over the last decade or so, in which previously ignored urban spaces are now being considered as valuable opportunities for wildlife conservation via natural meadow planting. This is a particularly welcome development – as well as increasing urban biodiversity, it can also help reduce air pollution and surface-water run-off, which could be invaluable in flood-prone areas. Surely every unused scrap of green space should be utilized like this – even motorway embankments and roundabouts.

Green streets

Leading the charge in this regreening initiative is designer Nigel Dunnett, who is helping to transform areas of Sheffield with the Grey to Green scheme, which began in 2014 and is still ongoing. The scheme has been a huge success, bringing a mile-long "green street" to an area along the inner-city dual carriageway, which was previously prone to flooding from the nearby Don River. The road is now reduced in lane size and has been planted with a multilayered scheme of perennials, grasses, and trees. Once established, these need little or no maintenance – a great selling point for many councils in these cash-strapped times, and a viable alternative to the usual high-maintenance expanses of tightly mown grass.

Now in demand across the country, and indeed the world, Dunnett and his team have brought colour, texture, and vibrancy to urban landscapes that might otherwise look bland, oppressive, or just plain municipal. There's the naturalistic Garden of Pooled Talents nestled amid a galvanized-metal art installation on the campus of the University of Sheffield; the bold, bright "flower fields" of the Olympic Meadows that burst into a riot of blue, orange, and yellow around the main stadium during the London 2012 Olympic Games; and the beautiful woodland planting scheme at Canal Reach, part of the extensive King's Cross regeneration project. Here, Dunnett has aimed to create the feel of a "multilayered forest", with a shady avenue of pin oaks that has perennials and shrubs beneath, offering seasonal interest. The idea, as in Sheffield, was to create "a garden on the street", using interlinked strips of flowerbeds on either side of the pavement, creating a welcome barrier from the road, and a much-appreciated sanctuary.

Lost spaces reclaimed

This approach to urban renewal has inspired further significant regenerations of what had been "lost" spaces, resulting in a truly diverse list of projects. At the Tower of London, the famous moat has been permanently reimagined as a wildflower meadow, with 20 million seeds sown to create a natural "Superbloom" display, with the aim of encouraging birds and pollinators to the area, as part of the 2022 celebrations for Queen Elizabeth II's Platinum Jubilee.

In the North, inspired by the success of the High Line public park in New York, the transformation of the formerly derelict Castlefield Viaduct in the heart of Manchester is a particularly exciting new development that will no doubt inspire others. Under the auspices of the National Trust, the Victorian railway bridge, which once linked industrial warehouses across the Rochdale Canal but closed in 1969, has been repurposed as a stunning "sky park", densely planted with ferns, grasses, and many herbaceous perennials that sway and glisten in the light.

Meanwhile, another masterful project has recently been completed in the centre of historic Cambridge: Europe's first "eco-mosque", a magnificent sustainable structure purpose-built for over 1,000 worshippers, supported internally by timber "trees" that echo the fan-vaulted ceiling of King's College Chapel. Shielding the building from the road is designer

The Islamic garden at the Cambridge Central Mosque, designed by Emma Clark, is built on the principles of paradise gardens, but with a sustainable twist

Emma Clark's beautifully planted Islamic garden. Following the traditional symbolic principles of paradise gardens, the four-part space is enclosed by evergreen yew hedges, with a circular water fountain at its centre and geometric patterns all around. The planting is naturalistic, contemporary, and thoughtful, including English crab apple trees for fruit and shade, and tulips – first cultivated in Turkey, the centre of the Ottoman Empire – to flower during Ramadan. Jewel-like colours mix with an abundance of green to provide an outstanding approach to the mosque that melds Islamic design with an English city setting and exudes a sense of calm and contemplation.

The development of all these urban gardens, installations, and planting schemes may seem incredibly modern, and yet the vision behind them is not so different from that of Victorian park designers such as John Claudius Loudon (see p.84). The overall intention remains the same: to provide a green oasis within what would otherwise be a forbidding city setting, where anyone – local, worker, or visitor – can find peace, serenity, and joy. With the added environmental incentive that is so urgent today, this movement is undoubtedly here to stay.

Going up

In an urban environment nothing is scarcer than garden space – that was, until gardeners realized they could look up! Rooftop gardens, high-rise gardens within buildings, even gardens growing up the side of buildings – the possibilities are now endless. And so, in recent years, many urban gardens have sprung up and up, in a neat design solution that provides natural city sanctuaries.

London's Barbican, the famous Brutalist arts and residential complex, was built in the 1960s–1970s with only uninspiring, high-maintenance lawns and flowerbeds in its "podium" or rooftop spaces. However, in 2013, the roof gardens were revolutionized, courtesy, again, of master urban designer Nigel Dunnett (see p.202), to introduce a contemporary and naturalistic planting scheme.

Recognizing that there were different microclimates throughout the site, Dunnett designed the scheme around three main plant communities that suit the same conditions: drought-tolerant grasses and perennials for full sun; additional shrubs and trees for year-round interest; and light woodland planting for part-shade. The result provides seasonal texture and colour against the stark urban backdrop, dramatically benefiting both residents and wildlife alike.

In nearby King's Cross, meanwhile, the Aga Khan Centre – a hub for Muslim culture – hosts a succession of tranquil rooftop spaces to represent the great diversity of Islamic gardens. While featuring many of the common elements – water, symmetry, star motifs, and the four-part layout representing the gardens of Paradise (known as *chahar bagh*) – the

spaces range in style and mood, from the sensory Courtyard of Harmony planted with pomegranate trees and thyme, to the Garden of Light, a minimal, contemplative space constructed from marble and patterned screens, with just a simple formation of trees to provide shade.

Both locations demonstrate what wonders can be achieved when seemingly redundant urban spaces are reimagined and revitalized.

Living walls

Adding greenery to drab concrete jungles doesn't just improve them aesthetically. It can also improve air quality, reduce temperatures, insulate buildings, absorb sound, boost biodiversity, and improve our mood. So when space is at a premium, the most effective way to implement this environmental life-saver is via the vertical garden, or living wall.

Having installed over 140 vertical gardens globally, award-winning French botanist Patrick Blanc is the expert, and his staggering 2009 creation at the Athenaeum hotel in London's Mayfair has understandably started a movement, with other living walls now blooming over numerous facades in the city, including the Rubens hotel in Victoria, Wimbledon's All England Tennis Club, and even Elephant & Castle and Edgware Road Underground stations. It's surely only a matter of time before London echoes Milan and grows its own "vertical forest" up a residential tower block!

As the demand for urban sanctuaries has grown, as the technology has improved (usually involving hydroponics and genius irrigation systems), and designers have learned how best to use and maintain the right plants, vertical and rooftop gardens have cropped up all over the country and, indeed, the world. London, Paris, Milan, China, and Singapore are leading the way, demonstrating that gardening skywards is now an integral part of building greener, happier, healthier urban spaces.

Patrick Blanc's living wall at the Athenaeum, installed in 2009, which stretches from street level to the 10th floor of the Mayfair hotel

King's Cross Gardens

A blend of naturalized parks, squares, and open spaces, the varied gardens at King's Cross reflect the area's history as a hub of trade and transport.

Bagley Walk, the elevated park at King's Cross Gardens, built on an old railway viaduct running alongside Regent's Canal

By the end of the 20th century, King's Cross in central London had become an industrial wasteland, popular with revellers but notorious for its high crime and unemployment levels. Now, the area has been transformed, and a series of individually designed contemporary gardens forms a tranquil green belt across this overwhelmingly urban setting. King's Cross is now a destination – a place to rest, reflect, meet, and be merry.

As with similar urban regeneration projects in Paris and New York, the King's Cross Gardens pay homage to the site's industrial heritage. In some of them, the planting is inspired by species that typically thrive in a city setting; in others, it is intended to convey a sense of heightened nature.

Urban haven

The largest green space in the roughly 26-acre plot is Lewis Cubitt Park, which was created by Townshend Landscape Architects with the classic lawns of London squares in mind. This is a contemporary version, moulded in such a way that its undulations form distinct areas. There are fountains and walkways, and trees and shrubs offer shade on hot days.

A nod to wild times at the warehouse club Bagley's, Bagley Walk overlooks Regent's Canal, Coal Drops Yard, and Camley Street Natural Park, a 2-acre nature reserve. Designer Dan Pearson's stunning planting both encourages biodiversity and softens the former railway viaduct, while surprisingly fruitful strawberry, fig, and liquorice plants encourage the foragers among us. This is a tranquil place, intended to attract wildlife and wildlife enthusiasts, and is reminiscent of the High Line elevated park in New York.

208

right *Jellicoe Gardens, where formal structure meets wild planting;* below *The open pavilion at the heart of Jellicoe Gardens, surrounded by oriental plane trees, is inspired by the columned entrances of Persian garden palaces*

Then we have Handyside Gardens, a Townshend–Pearson collaboration and a beautiful pocket park inspired by the pattern of the railway lines that previously criss-crossed the space. Naturalistic planting re-creates the wildness that ensues when nature reclaims derelict tracks: asters and multi-stemmed willows weave their way through a multitude of various grasses. The adjoining Wharf Road Gardens, curving along the canal, also echo former railway tracks. Here, the abundant planting is contained within weathered steel frames, emphasizing the site's industrial nature. The gardens lead to Granary Square, a vibrant space with more than 1,000 waterjets that spurt at random, catching out children and adults alike to great hilarity. This interactive playfulness and urban-beach feel is typical of parks in Paris, such as the Parc André Citroën.

Persian paradise

The most fascinating space at King's Cross, however, is the Persian-themed Jellicoe Gardens, designed by Tom Stuart-Smith. With a grand pavilion at its centre, the garden is a fusion of English herbaceous planting and what Stuart-Smith cites as his inspiration, the 16th-century garden of Bagh-e Fin, in Kashan, Iran. A rill runs through the glorious terrace planting, connecting the whole design, while a bubbling water feature creates movement and gentle sound. Jellicoe Gardens is a tribute to Geoffrey Jellicoe (see p.156), a former resident of the area who was renowned for his use of water in garden design. It is a masterpiece, and one that serves as a gateway to the Islamic gardens of the Aga Khan Centre (see p.204) – a whole new horticultural journey.

Looking forward

"If you grow contented plants you will find contentment yourself."

Beth Chatto, Gardens Illustrated, *1995*

The role our gardens could play in mitigating the overall effects of climate change has never been more significant than it is now. As we move further into the 21st century and the climate warms, the way we garden, the plants we grow, and the materials we use will need to change if we are to protect and increase biodiversity, conserve water, and reduce carbon emissions.

Making the changes

The RHS is leading the way, demonstrating this new sustainable vision in their own gardens, and offering advice on what we can do in ours. Swapping our lush herbaceous borders for a drought-tolerant Mediterranean palette is key. Our desire for verdant lawns will also need to change due to the maintenance and water required; climate-aware gardeners have long been shifting towards meadow planting instead to draw in pollinators. As far back as the 1970s, natural scientist Miriam Rothschild created a magnificent wildflower meadow at her Ashton Wold estate in Northamptonshire, and provided a bespoke seed mix for King Charles III to use at Highgrove (see p.180).

Peat usage has dropped markedly in recent years, which is to be applauded (extracting peat from natural bogs not only destroys habitats, but releases huge amounts of carbon), but we can go further, avoiding chemicals, planting trees, making our own compost, and saving water by switching, as the RHS Mains to Rains campaign recommends, from using mains water to rainwater in our gardens.

Right plant, right place

The biggest transition we must make, however, is adopting Beth Chatto's mantra, the keystone to ecological gardening: "right plant, right place". In other words, choosing plants naturally adapted to their conditions. Although critics have decried the idea for denying us roses and colourful

borders, a visit to any RHS garden, Beth Chatto's garden at Elmstead in Essex (see p.178), or Denmans in Sussex (see p.152) demonstrates what stunning displays can be achieved with this method. Indeed, the Dry Garden at RHS Hyde Hall in Essex is dominated by cool greys and pale greens but bursts into spectacular colour from Mediterranean, Australian, and African flowers in summer – and it has not been watered in 22 years!

We are certainly not short of inspiration. The trend for naturalistic planting has been growing since the 1980s, and today our top garden designers – particularly Piet Oudolf, Dan Pearson, Nigel Dunnett, James Hitchmough, and Christopher Bradley-Hole – are showing us how to create beautiful schemes with

these new plant choices that are both ecologically sound and aesthetically diverse. Meanwhile, the many urban regreening projects (see p.202) cropping up all over the world are an exciting glimpse of future possibilities.

So yes, the way we garden and the plants we use will certainly have to transform over the coming years, but one thing will never change. Gardens are our refuge, our sanctuary, the places where, in a fast-paced, digital world, we can slow down and reconnect with the earth – quite literally ground ourselves – to find peace, calm, and tranquillity. If we look after our gardens in a responsible, sustainable way, they can help us in return to restore not only the natural world, but our mind and spirit too.

More than 400 species of drought-resilient grasses, shrubs, and herbaceous perennials fill the borders of the Dry Garden at RHS Hyde Hall, Essex

CASE STUDY

Lowther Castle

After nearly a century of neglect, these austere ruins are being brought back to life with a modern, naturalistic planting scheme that befits the incredible setting.

The Tapestry Garden in the courtyard of Lowther Castle, where linear clipped hornbeam hedges contrast with moody perennials

Cumbria's Lowther Castle, a 19th-century castellated mansion with gardens designed by local landscape architect Thomas Mawson, was abandoned in 1936 after the profligate 5th Earl of Lonsdale, Hugh Lowther, lost the family fortune. By the 1960s, only the outer walls remained, and the gardens had been overtaken by a chicken farm, pig pens, and Christmas trees. But Lowther Castle now has a future, thanks to an exciting redevelopment programme masterminded by garden designer Dan Pearson and the Lowther family.

Pearson looked to the gardens of Ninfa in Italy for inspiration. There, nature appears to have reclaimed a medieval village, and glassy streams trickle magically through the grounds. Pearson's Garden-in-the-Ruins echoes this approach, with billowing climbing roses threaded through the castle ruins, while the walls form a backdrop to textural and floral planting within the spaces.

Fusing old and new

On the castle's south side, the Tapestry Garden pays tribute to Mawson's formal scheme, but in a contemporary way. Dark-flowered perennials and grasses accentuate the symmetry of the building, while hornbeam columns enclose the space and create intimacy.

Inspired by the tale of "Sleeping Beauty" (or "Briar Rose"), the Rose Garden features more than 1,000 eglantine roses and perennials, including white *Geranium macrorrhizum*, planted in the shape of a rose. Sweeping paths through the woodland lead to the romantic Rock Garden, a haven of mossy rocks and clever planting, then on to the Japanese Garden, which has an otherworldly atmosphere. But the masterstroke has to be the wildflower meadows flanking the South Lawns.

Though it is far from finished, Lowther Castle's magical garden, steeped in history, is both intimate and vast, tranquil and overwhelming. The rhythm Pearson has created bodes well for the future of this long-term project – indeed, it is already outstanding.

Meandering wildflower meadows and woodland surround Dan Pearson's Parterre Garden at Lowther Castle in Cumbria.

Index

Glossary

Allée A landscaped pathway bordered by trees or tall planting.

Apiary An area where honey beehives are kept.

Arboretum A garden of trees or shrubs.

Arbour A shelter often created by trees or shrubbery trained over a wooden or metal structure or trellis.

Bosquet A formal plantation of trees.

Cottage ornée A stylized rustic building, typically seen as part of 18th-century landscape garden designs.

Exedra A seating area in the style of Classical gardens of Greece and Rome.

Fastigiate A tree or shrub with branches parallel to the main stem.

Finial A decorative element at the top of a spire.

Grotto An ornamental structure shape like a small cave, a feature of 18th-century landscape gardens.

Ha-ha A sunken wall or fence to contain livestock, placed so as not to interrupt the view of the garden or landscape beyond.

Hortus conclusus Mediaeval walled garden, from the Latin meaning "enclosed garden".

Knot garden Formal garden design with mediaeval origins, flowerbeds separated by low clipped hedges.

Labyrinth garden Mediaeval style of garden with meandering pathways enclosed by hedges.

Parterre garden Formal design of flowerbeds, low hedges, and pathways arranged to form a pattern, which originated in 16th-century France.

Patte d'oie Three or more straight paths radiating out from a central point, from the French for "goose's foot".

Pavilion An ornamental building in a park or garden.

Pergola An archway or roofed, trellis structure, over which climbing plants can be trained.

Permaculture An agricultural system based on the principle of working with the natural environment.

Pleaching Branches of shrubs or trees woven into a lattice to form a living fence.

Terrace A flat paved or turfed area extending from a house, associated with Italian Renaissance garden design.

Topiary The art of pruning trees and shrubs such as yew or box into ornamental shapes.

Author acknowledgments

First, a huge thank-you to DK for this opportunity to write my first book. It's a journey that would have been impossible without the initial concept by Chris Young, and the endless support of Ruth O'Rourke. Thanks also to the remarkable team that enthusiastically gathered around me; all are stars and need to be acknowledged: Geoff Borin, Emily Hedges, Maxine Pedliham, Victoria Pyke, Lucy Sienkowska, and Barbara Zuniga. And special thanks must go to the marvellous and always patient Holly Kyte, who daily bit her lip and patiently guided my words and tangential thoughts, and without whom this book would have remained a pipe dream.

Many thanks, also, to my superb friends and colleagues at Cardiff University, in particular Dr Zbig Sobiesierski for taking a chance on the excitable lecturer who proposed a whole new range of courses when many were being closed! Thank you, also, to a variety of garden historians, particularly Professor (now Emeritus) Timothy Mowl, who inspired me with his enthusiasm, intellectual rigour, and love of gossip, and the late Professor Michael Liversidge, whom I will always admire for his support, his precision, and his encyclopaedic knowledge of art and culture, and for defining what constitutes a true gentleman. Also to my fellow students at Bristol University, including the marvellous Sue Shephard and the ever-impressive Katie Campbell, for our shared passions and memorable trips around the gardens of Paris and Florence. There are too many others to name, but I have hugely appreciated everyone's input.

Lastly, I must thank my late grandfather, who sparked this garden passion in me as a child, and the much-missed instinctive gardener who was my darling mum, who continued that work. My family today remains a never-ending source of support and inspiration and fun.

Publisher acknowledgments

DK would like to thank Martin Copeland and Manpreet Kaur for picture research assistance, Kathryn Glendenning for proofreading, and Helen Peters for indexing.

References

To access a comprehensive bibliography and list of references supporting the text in this book, please visit: www.dk.com/englands-gardens-biblio

Picture credits

The publisher would like to thank the following sources for their kind permission to reproduce their photographs:

Key: t = top b = bottom l = left r = right

Page 2: Andrew Montgomery; **4-5 GAP Photos**/Abigail Rex; **7 Jonathan Buckley**; **8** tl Photograph by RHS Lindley Library/**Camera Press**, tr **Alamy**/Kay Ringwood, bl © Mallett Gallery, London, UK / **Bridgeman Images**, br **Alamy**/VTR; **11** The Stapleton Collection/**Bridgeman Images**; **13** l **Alamy**/Charles Walker Collection, r © British Library Board. All Rights Reserved/**Bridgeman Images**; **15 Alamy**/agefotostock; **16 Alamy**/Skyscan Photolibrary; **17 Cambridge, Trinity College, Crewe Collection** - courtesy of The Master and Fellows of Trinity College, Cambridge; **18-19 Alamy**/robertharding; **20-21 Clive Nichols**; **21** br **Alamy**/Heritage Image Partnership Ltd.; **22-23 GAP Photos**/Charles Hawes; **25 Mike Calnan and Mark Smeaton**; **26 Alamy**/Jimlop Collection; **29** t **Alamy**/Topographical Collection, b © Image; Crown Copyright: **UK Government Art Collection**; **30 Alamy**/Urban Napflin; **31** t © British Library Board. All Rights Reserved/**Bridgeman Images**, b **Alamy**/Architecture 2000; **33 Alamy**/The National Trust Photolibrary; **34 GAP Photos**/Richard Bloom; **36 Clive Nichols**; **39** © Ashmolean Museum/**Bridgeman Images**; **40** © Dulwich Picture Gallery/**Bridgeman Images**; **43** t **Alamy**/Antiqua Print Gallery, b **MMGI**/Marianne Majerus; **44-45 MMGI**/Marianne Majerus; **45** r **Alamy**/incamerastock; **47 Alamy**/Tim Gainey; **49 and 50 Bridgeman Images**; **51 Alamy**/Yorkshire Pics; **52-53 MMGI**/Andrew Lawson, **54-55 Clive Nichols; 54** b **MMGI**/Andrew Lawson; **57** t and b © British Library Board. All Rights Reserved/**Bridgeman Images**; **58** t and b **Alamy**/The National Trust Photolibrary; **62 Alamy**/Zoonar GmbH; **64** t **Alamy**/Manor Photography, b **Alamy**/The National Trust Photoblibrary; **66-67 Alamy**/National Trust Photolibrary; **69** © Detroit Institute of Arts/**Bridgeman Images**; **70** © **Victoria and Albert Museum, London**; **73 Alamy**/Artokoloro; **74 Bridgeman Images**; **75 Alamy**/Rob Cousins; **77** t **Alamy**/Magite Historic, b **Clive Nichols**; **78** l **Clive Nichols**, r **GAP Photos**/Clive Nichols; **79** l **Alamy**/Anne Gilbert; **81** t The Stapleton Collection/**Bridgeman Images**, b **Alamy**/The National Trust Photolibrary; **83 MMGI**/Marianne Majerus; **87 Alamy**/Florilegius; **88 Alamy**/Artokoloro; **91 with permission of the Trustees, Royal Botanic Garden Edinburgh**; **92 Alamy**/Jacky Parker; **94-95 Dreamstime**/Yujie Chen; **97** © **TfL from the London Transport Museum collection**; **99 courtesy of Dorking Museum**; **100-101 GAP Photos**/Carole Drake – Owners:

William and Marianne Cartwright-Hignett; **103** t and b **MMGI**/Marianne Majerus; **105 GAP Photos**/Carole Drake; **107** t **Annabel Watts**, b photo © Chris Beetles Ltd, London/**Bridgeman Images**; **108 and 109 Annabel Watts**; **111** t **GAP Photos**/John Glover, b **GAP Photos**/Jonathan Buckley; **112-113 MMGI**/Marianne Majerus; **115** © **Bath & North East Somerset Council** www.bathintime.co.uk; **117 Bridgeman Images** © Estate of Duncan Grant. All rights reserved, DACS 2022; **118-119 Jonathan Buckley**; **120** t **MMGI**/Marianne Majerus, b © **National Trust Images**/Eva Nemeth; **121 Jonathan Buckley**; **123** t © Benton End House and Garden Trust, b © Estate of Cedric Morris. All rights reserved 2022/**Bridgeman Images**; **125 Alamy**/Amoret Tanner Collection; **126 Imperial War Museum**; **129 Royal Collection Trust**/© His Majesty King Charles III 2022; **130 Getty**/Picture Post; **131 Getty**/Popperfoto; **133 Mary Evans Picture Library**; **135 Getty**/Culture Club; **136 Getty**/Buyenlarge; **138 Getty**/Science & Society Picture Library; **139 Alamy**/thislife pictures; **141 Getty**/Mirrorpix; **143 RIBA Collections**/Architectural Press Archive; **144 RIBA Collections**/Henk Snoek; **146-147 Alamy**/The National Trust Photolibrary; **148** t ©**National Trust Images**/Dennis Gilbert, b ©**National Trust Images**/Stuart Cox; **151 The John Brookes-Denmans Foundation**; **152 GAP Photos**/Andrea Jones; **154-155 MMGI**/Marianne Majerus; **157 MMGI**/Marianne Majerus; **158** t **Sabina Rüber**, b **MMGI**/Marianne Majerus; **161 GAP Photos**/Highgrove – A. Butler; **163 GAP Photos**/Rob Whitworth; **164-165 GAP Photos**/Richard Bloom; **166** t **GAP Photos**/Charles Hawes, b **GAP Photos**/Richard Bloom; **167 GAP Photos**/Richard Bloom; **169 Country Life**/Future Publishing Ltd.; **171-173 MMGI**/Marianne Majerus; **175 Kim Wilkie**; **176 Andrew Lawson**; **178-179 MMGI**/Marianne Majerus; **180 GAP Photos**/Highgrove – Robert Smith; **182 and 183 GAP Photos**/Highgrove – A.Butler; **185 The Newt in Somerset**; **187-189 Clive Nichols**; **191** t Simon Brown/**The Interior Archive**, b **MMGI**/Marianne Majerus; **193 Clive Nichols** – Horatio's Garden South West at The Duke of Cornwall Spinal Treatment Centre at Salisbury District Hospital. Designer: Cleeve West; **195** t and br **MMGI**/Marianne Majerus, bl **Getty**/ Steve Pyke; **196 and 197 MMGI**/Marianne Majerus; **199** © **Britt Willoughby Dyer** for Yeo Valley Organic; **200 MMGI**/Marianne Majerus; **201 GAP Photos**/Clive Nichols; **203 GAP Photos**/Howard Rice – Landscape design: Urquhart & Hunt; **205 The Athenaeum Hotel and Residences**; **206-209** © **John Sturrock/KCCLP**; **211 Jason Ingram**; **212-213 Claire Takacs**; **214-215 Gap Photos**/Carole Drake.

Cover images Artwork copyright © David de las Heras, 2023

About the author

Stephen Parker is a garden historian who has been lecturing at Cardiff University for nearly 12 years. As well as visiting over 100 gardens every year, he is also known to take detours to photograph modernist or Art Deco houses tucked away nearby. Having worked for Terence Conran's Habitat in the 1980s, Stephen established his own store in Brighton, Arkitekt, one of a small group of retailers bringing the best of design from around the world to the English high street. After many years working in London, he returned to Cardiff in 2000 and studied for a master's degree in garden history at Bristol University, joining a fascinating group of garden historians that had gathered there. A keen enthusiast for all that is modern, Stephen embraces people and products that are breaking new ground; but he retains a fascination for all aspects of garden history, from scandalous gossip to its cultural and social context. A passionate Welshman, Stephen has travelled extensively and is partial to a grand story or two. He can often be found among the topiary with his AirPods on loud.

Editors Holly Kyte, Victoria Pyke
Project Designer Geoff Borin
Picture Researcher Emily Hedges
Jacket Illustrator David de las Heras
Jacket Design Concept Matt Cox
Consultant Gardening Publisher Chris Young

DK
Project Editor Lucy Sienkowska
Senior Designer Barbara Zuniga
Editorial Manager Ruth O'Rourke
Design Manager Marianne Markham
Senior Production Editor Tony Phipps
Senior Production Controller Stephanie McConnell
Editorial Assistant Charlotte Beauchamp
Jacket Coordinator Jasmin Lennie
DTP and Design Coordinator Heather Blagden
Art Director Maxine Pedliham
Publishing Director Katie Cowan

First published in Great Britain in 2023 by
Dorling Kindersley Limited
DK, One Embassy Gardens, 8 Viaduct Gardens,
London, SW11 7BW

The authorised representative in the EEA is
Dorling Kindersley Verlag GmbH. Arnulfstr. 124,
80636 Munich, Germany

A CIP catalogue record for this book
is available from the British Library.
ISBN: 978-0-2416-1157-9

Printed and bound in Malaysia

For the curious
www.dk.com

MIX
Paper | Supporting
responsible forestry
FSC™ C018179

This book was made with Forest Stewardship Council™ certified paper – one small step in DK's commitment to a sustainable future. **For more information go to** www.dk.com/our-green-pledge